the second
epistle to the
Corinthians

the second
epistle to the
Corinthians

H.C.G. MOULE D.D.

CHRISTIAN LITERATURE CRUSADE

Fort Washington, Pennsylvania 19034

CHRISTIAN LITERATURE CRUSADE
Fort Washington, Pennsylvania 19034

CANADA
1440 Mackay Street, Montreal, Quebec

This edition 1976 by special arrangement
with the British publisher Pickering and Inglis Ltd.

ISBN 0-87508-359-5

To

MY DEAR

FATHER AND MOTHER

LOVERS OF THE WORD OF LIFE

SAINTS' COMMUNION

He wants not friends that hath Thy love,
  And may converse and walk with Thee,
And with Thy saints here and above,
  With whom for ever I must be.

In the Communion of Saints
  Is wisdom, safety and delight,
And when my heart declines and faints,
  It's raised by their heart and light!

Before Thy throne we daily meet
  As joint-petitioners to Thee;
In spirit we each other greet,
  And shall again each other see.

—RICHARD BAXTER, 1616-1691

Preface Editorial

DR. WALTER LOCK has placed on record of Bishop Handley Moule that 'his writings form the most spiritual and scholarly expression in his generation of the Christian faith as held by Evangelical churchmen, proud of the Reformers, and holding that their teaching is "the most loyal in proportion and emphasis to the New Testament standard".' There is, moreover, an unmistakable atmosphere of Catholicity, as distinct from Catholicism, about his works which those who read will recognize. Bishop Handley Moule's writings are indeed classic examples of orthodox Exposition. It is therefore a privilege in our generation to preserve what he has written, and, at the present juncture, a responsibility which may not be evaded.

Dr. Handley Moule was appointed Norrisian Professor of Divinity at Cambridge in 1899. After his Inaugural Lecture, in the first academic year of his appointment he lectured on the *Second Epistle to the Corinthians*. The Lecture Notes, which were somewhat incomplete, were laid aside. But they are represented in this book, in the Introduction, and in his detailed treatment of the text of this epistle, now published for the first time, a full generation after his departure. Together with the lecture notes there are other portions of his characteristic writings on the same epistle. The poignant Latin footnotes are taken from the Greek Testament which was his daily companion for the greater part of his episcopate at Durham, (1901-1920), where his name is a memorial.

The epistle was treated in the first instance as a series of lectures to students. The lecturer's object was to enable the younger students in the theological school 'so to read the Epistles of St. Paul as adequately to grasp the often subtle and complex sequence of thought, and to present to themselves in a satisfactory way the complex drift and argument of extended passages'. Others besides students will find the same need. The lecturer's purpose as thus expressed in the Inaugural Lecture may be fulfilled by reading straight through the text and paraphrase only, in this volume. A careful translation of the text is given in heavy type and connexions of thought are found in lighter type. Close attention is given to the sections and paragraphs.

The Apostle and the author would surely rejoice if this book also proves a help to missionaries and translators. It seems that this is the only extant epistle of the greatest of all missionary travellers actually written *en route*. As regards translation it is worth recording that Archdeacon Guillebaud of Ruanda, in the heart of Africa, when asked which was the most difficult book in the New Testament to translate, replied, 'The Second Epistle to the Corinthians'. When this Epistle was completed and the time came for its delivery to the Church a huge congregation gathered together. The epistle was then read aloud, and right through, to the native church. When the last words were finished a silent awe and wonder came over the vast assembly to hear such a marvellous range of spiritual experience expressed for the first time in their own language.

This Epistle is also a storehouse of 'moving and ravishing texts' for the preacher. 'What an admirable Epistle is the second to the Corinthians! how full of affections! he joys and he is sorry, he grieves, and he glories. Never was there such care of a flock expressed, save in the great Shepherd of the fold, who first shed tears over Jerusalem, and afterwards blood. Therefore this care may be learned there, and then woven into Sermons, which will make them appear exceeding reverend and holy.' George Herbert's precepts are exemplified in several of Handley Moule's sanctified writings which have been used to fill in the homiletic portions of this book. There is indeed an affinity between them of spiritual scholarship and style. Neither is 'dated'. Both are timeless through possession of 'the Unction spiritual'. Handley Moule can also, on occasion, be singularly epigrammatic, and even prophetic.

A further word may be added about style. Handley Moule's style was highly individual, and would have been distinctive at any time. Its peculiarities and flavour, it may be said, are not in keeping with the taste of the present generation. But in a previous generation his language was labelled, rather inaccurately, as 'Elizabethan', and now he seems to have a message for the hour! Normally he is not specially helpful to new converts, but growth in grace brings growth in understanding, till, for many, his writings become a spiritual norm of that which is best. In good company with the Authorized Version his words retain their ancient power.

To return. Readers of all kinds, as well as preachers, will discover authoritative treatment of themes which are of immediate interest and abiding significance in the Christian life. The Epistle deals with principles Evangelistic and Pastoral (Ch. III). It contains passages relating closely to life after death, and here through scholarship and affliction Bishop Moule is a safe guide (Ch. VI and VII). There is moreover found in it a passage of cardinal importance in dealing with the Atonement (Ch. VIII). In its latter sections Christian Stewardship of money is treated in the most extended passage in all Scripture (Ch. XII and XIII). At the end we have the fragrant theme 'Sufficient for thee the grace of Me' (Ch. XVI). What Handley Moule wrote he expressed in his life, and has declared to be for us all.

In regard to the volume as a whole the reader may be referred to his *Romans*, and *Ephesian*, *Philippian* and *Colossian Studies* on which it has been modelled. Those who know these expositions will never part with them. Those who have a family of them will doubtless welcome the youngest—'as of one born out of due time'. It may indeed be claimed that Handley Moule's work on *Second Corinthians* represents that rendering which he made so much his own in its latest and most mature expression, disclosing spiritual insight as faithful scholarship's senior partner. To appreciate this the work must be read right through. In the latter part, particularly in St. Paul's Apologia, we seem to go for a walk with the blessed Apostle and his disciple, and are privileged to overhear their holy converse. It took a pastor to

2

write the Epistle, and it takes a pastor to interpret the Apostle.

After the Paraphrase will be found a series of Appendices, largely consecutive. *Appendix A* contains The Warden of Keble's contribution to the *Dictionary of National Biography*, quoted above, and acquaints us with the author. This most personal epistle became an integral part of the Bishop's life. *Abeunt studia in mores*. Learning leavens life. *Appendix B* includes relevant passages from the Inaugural Lecture, in which the author himself prefaces his work on the Epistle and indicates his views of Inspiration. The first two Appendices may well be read before the main part of the book is begun. *Appendix C* explains how the book has been put together, and sets out the editorial treatment of *The Lecturer's MS.*, *The Greek Testament*, and *The Other Writings*, including a *Table of Editorial Material*. *Appendix D* deals with historical questions connected with the Epistle.

Bishop Handley Moule was recognized and is still generally recognized as a conservative scholar of note. In dealing with his autographs there has been independently and insistently borne in upon me a series of thoughts in connexion with the Inspiration of Holy Scripture. I have therefore tried to explain some of these thoughts in the concluding passages of several of the Appendices, adding at the end an extended note on *Coalescent Inspiration*. Anything which will help us to define our terms will enable us the better to form a right judgment on this vital subject.

Special thanks must be expressed to Mr. E. C. H. Moule, my uncle, for diverse 'helps'; to Canon C. W. J. Bowles, Principal of Ridley Hall, Cambridge, for his careful custody of Bishop Moule's MSS.; to Dr. F. F. Bruce of Manchester, John Rylands Professor, for effective encouragement and assistance from time to time; to the Rev. A. Gelston, M.A., of Keble College, Curate of Chipping Norton, for his devoted and scholarly typing of the whole book; to the Printers and Publishers for their care and skill. Others who have helped in many ways—members of the family, friends, and fellow students of the younger generation will have their reward when this book is at last in their hands.

Mrs. de Vere, the Bishop's daughter, has quite recently gone to be with Christ. Very graciously she gave me at an early stage the MS. of the Lecture Notes. Later she supplied the original for the frontispiece photograph, taken in 1910, and gave me her enthusiastic support.

Above all our thanks to the Author, particularly for leaving his parchments behind!

Having received my great-uncle's blessing as a boy I now dedicate this volume to his god-son, my Father, with my Mother, in the Communion of Saints. Inspired by my wife, carried through in a country Rectory, and extended over a period of 9 years this work has been a spiritual mainstay, altering life for one who is 'less than the least' of the author's disciples. Now as Bible Year closes the vessel is launched, freighted with consolation and committed to the swelling waters of The Spirit.

To GOD be the Glory!

Thanks be to GOD. Grace be to men.

To all lovers of Handley Moule and his writings—

Greetings in Christ Jesus.

A. W. HANDLEY MOULE,

Woolhampton Rectory,

Nr. Reading

All Saints
1961

I thought I saw to-night very fully in Zech. iv. how it is that GOD takes men as instruments for His Church's good. Here is the candlestick, but the oil is brought out by pipes. Now the olive-trees represent instruments, such as men that have gifts, and their gifts are the olive-berries on yonder trees. The Holy Spirit pours the oil out of these trees with the pipes, and so the whole Church gets the good of these gifts. In this way I see how it is that good books are made use of by God, they are just those olive-trees and their berries. Lord, let me be such by all I write. I have a drawing of that vision in my room. Let it ever remind me of how God may use everything I write.

—ANDREW A. BONAR. *Diary and Letters.*

Contents

THE CHOICE OF THE EPISTLE

THE choice of this particular Book of the Holy Scriptures, the Second Epistle to the Corinthians, was determined in my mind by several considerations. On the whole, that Epistle has been, comparatively speaking, somewhat neglected as a field of study in itself. Yet few great portions of the New Testament have a more distinctive character—I might almost say, so living are its pages, a more powerful individuality. No doubt it cannot be studied without frequent reference to its great predecessor, the First Epistle, written so short a time before, and attached to it by so many links. Yet in important respects the Second Epistle stands apart, a thing of its own kind, full of phenomena peculiar to itself.

—From The Inaugural Lecture.

(See further Appendix B, page 136).

THE STUDY OF THE EPISTLE

THE first thing necessary is to obtain an impression of the Epistle as a whole. It should be read, as we receive the letters that we receive today, straight through—and perhaps more than once—from beginning to end. We should try to read it as if we had never seen it before, and paying no attention to the divisions into chapters and verses. Then we should ask ourselves what help we need for the better understanding of it. Probably our difficulties will be many. First—and this may be peculiarly the case with the Second Epistle to the Corinthians—we shall fail to grasp the historical situation.   Secondly, we shall find ourselves unfamiliar with the writer's religious outlook, and so imperfectly understand his moral and doctrinal teaching. Thirdly, there will be many places where we shall find his language obscure; and that, either because, as in St. Paul's case, of his peculiarities as a writer, or because the A.V. and R.V., in aiming at a faithful translation of his words, shrink from the paraphrase which is often necessary for the understanding of his meaning.

H. L. GOUDGE,
Westminster Commentary (adapted)

INTRODUCTION

For the author's purpose in the Introduction see Appendix B, p. 137. For the Lecture Notes on which this Introduction is based and for their Editorial treatment, see Appendix C. 1 (b), and Appendix C.3, p. 151.

INTRODUCTION

I

Authenticity

The authenticity of St. Paul's Second Epistle to the Corinthians scarcely admits of question. Whether we take up this sacred letter as a single composition or whether we think of it as two or three separate letters pieced together makes no difference here. There is a general and practically unanimous consensus of opinion that this portion of Holy Scripture is without question the composition of the great apostle. It is a simple literary fact, as we shall have constant occasion to note, that the first and second Epistles are closely interlaced. The first Epistle is recognized by all as the work of St. Paul. And as we read through the second Epistle we find that, even more than in the first, the fervent spirit of none other than the Apostle Paul himself breathes in all its phrases and is disclosed at each abrupt turn of thought and feeling. Only a defective appreciation of personality, carrying with it an inability to distinguish the real from the artificial, can lead to any other conclusion than that the Epistle is genuine. Thus in common with the representatives of every influential school of criticism we regard the Pauline authorship as unimpeached and unimpeachable.

In considering the epistle further it is interesting and instructive to note that while the internal evidence is so powerful there is a remarkable scarcity of early reference from external sources. Clement, writing from Rome (c. 97 A.D.) makes an indirect reference to the Epistle. 'Through zeal and envy,' he says, 'the most faithful and righteous pillars of the Church have been persecuted'. And then he details the sufferings of the apostle in words which faintly echo St. Paul's personal catalogue in 2 Cor. xi. 23f. 'Seven times he was in bonds,' Clement says, 'he was whipped and stoned: he preached both in the east and in the west, leaving behind him the glorious report of his faith'.[1]

---

[1] First Epistle of St. Clement to the Corinthians ch. v.

Polycarp writing a little later (*c.* 111 A.D.) quotes loosely from 2 Cor. iv. 14 when he says, 'He that raised Christ up from the dead shall also raise up us in like manner if we do His will'.[1] He distinctly quotes from 2 Cor. v. 10 when he says that 'we ought also to forgive others, for we are all in the sight of our Lord and God, and must all stand before the judgement-seat of Christ, and shall every one give an account of himself'.[2] But apart from these scanty references there is no mention of the Epistle in Ignatius (*c.* 110 A.D.) or any of the early fathers. Later references are abundant,[3] but the early testimony, as we have already said, is powerful internally but meagre externally. It seems as though The Spirit, who so evidently inspired the words of the Epistle, considered that they bore their own marks of authenticity and therefore needed little further support in the disposal of Divine Providence.

II

The Place from which

The place from which the Epistle was sent was evidently Macedonia. St. Paul had passed through Troas into Macedonia (ii. 12, 13). There he had been met by Titus (vii. 5, 6) and there he had been making a collection for the Jerusalem poor. He refers to this collection in general terms when he writes of 'the grace of God bestowed on the churches of Macedonia, how that in a great trial of affliction, the abundance of their joy, and their deep poverty, abounded unto the riches of their liberality' (viii. 1, 2). This collection, moreover, was not only being made in Macedonia but also had already been made in Achaia, which included Corinth. So, writing in his Second Epistle to the Corinthians, St. Paul says, 'I glory on your behalf to them of

---

[1] St. Polycarp to the Philippians ch. ii.
[2] Ibid., ch. vi.
[3] The Epistle to Diognetus (cent. 2) ch. 5 is inspired by 2 Cor. vi. 8-10. The writer speaks of those to whom he writes as 'unknown and condemned', 'put to death and raised to life', 'poor but making many rich', etc. 2 Corinthians is listed in the heretic Marcion's Canon (cent. 2) and in the Muratorian Canon which was by way of an orthodox answer to Marcion. In Irenaeus, Tertullian and Clement of Alexandria there are full references to the Epistle.

Macedonia, that Achaia hath been prepared for a year past; and your zeal hath stirred up very many of them' (ix. 2). A little further on he envisages the possibility of some of those of Macedonia coming with him when the time should come for him to go on to Corinth (ix. 4).

From these references we gather that the Second Epistle was written somewhere in Macedonia in one of the churches or mission-stations along the road from Philippi to Thessalonica. St. Paul was at this time confirming the churches which he had previously founded and making his way through Macedonia, down into Achaia and so on to Corinth. He had just spent about three years in Ephesus, from whence he had written his First Epistle. Now he writes from Macedonia to prepare for his arrival in person at Corinth.

Here we may note that the Peshitta or Syriac version, which is a translation of the Greek, indicates that it was written at Philippi. This it will be seen corresponds with the subscription to the A.V.—'written from Philippi a city of Macedonia by Titus and Lucas'; and Dr. Plumptre, in Ellicott's *General Commentary*, referring to ch. viii. 16-22 says that in this case the subscription may be regarded as 'a legitimate inference from the data furnished by the Epistle'. Philippi would certainly be the first place in Macedonia from which it could have been written, and we may perhaps imagine the Apostle as beginning the letter there and finishing it as he passed from one station to another along the road. R. B. Rackham in his *Commentary on Acts* makes the interesting observation that 'it seems to have been written from time to time like a diary', and suggests how different sections of the Epistle were written as St. Paul travelled through Macedonia, and how it was finally dispatched from Thessalonica. Some such explanation may lie behind the great division of the Epistle which we make at ch. vii. 2.[1]

---

[1] See R. B. Rackham, *Westminster Commentary on Acts*, p. 371. For the division of the Epistle at vii. 2 and for its earlier and later characteristics, see ch. x, Retrospect and Review.

III

Date and Time

The date and time at which the Epistle was written we may attempt to fix by St. Luke's detailed reference to St. Paul's movements in Acts xx. 1-6. After St. Paul had passed through Macedonia into Greece to Corinth, he stayed there three months. During this short visit he composed his great Epistle to the Romans—early in 58 A.D.[1] Then, returning into Macedonia, he came back to Philippi, from where he eventually sailed 'after the days of unleavened bread', or after Easter (Acts xx. 6). If St. Paul sailed from Philippi after Easter of 58 A.D. he must have passed down through Macedonia sometime between September and December of the previous year. We may, therefore, state with some assurance that his Second Epistle was written to the Corinthians *c*. Oct. 57 A.D.

Let us try briefly to envisage the political setting, and the Roman world of that day. It was the third year of Nero. Following his predecessors Claudius and Caligula he had inherited through them the imperial wealth and stability of Tiberius and Augustus. Not yet had he shown his character, though recently Poppaea has caught the prince in the net of her baneful influence. Tiberius had established the Roman power in the North against the Germanic tribes. Now Domitius Corbulo was just resuming the war with Parthia and preparing to penetrate the highlands of Armenia. Meanwhile not only was the empire expanding but a new religion was beginning to make its way into the highest circles. The influence of Poppaea had hardly begun when in the very same year, A.D. 57, Pomponia Graecina the wife of Aulus Plautius, conqueror of Britain, became a Christian.

It was only twenty-seven years after the Crucifixion. What a flood of light that sheds on the Epistle St. Paul was writing! How near it brings The Christ who shines so gloriously through its pages! St. Paul in His Name was engaged in a desperate spiritual contest, and the Roman Empire was even then entering on a series of ideological convulsions which led eventually to the

[1] In conformity with the author's *Expositor's Romans* which follows Lewin's *Fasti Sacri*.

triumph of the Christian faith. Two mighty religious forces had begun their contest for the soul of the Empire, while St. Paul was calmly writing from Macedonia—'Having therefore these promises, beloved, let us cleanse ourselves from all defilement of the flesh and spirit, perfecting holiness in the fear of God' (ch. vii. 1).

IV
The Place to which

The place to which St. Paul was writing was restored and 'Roman' Corinth—a great city of commerce and pleasure. Above it towered the Acrocorinthus, the citadel of Corinth, rising abruptly to a height of 2,000 feet and casting a vast shadow across the plain from its base, where the new city was built and was spreading out its suburbs. The earlier Greek city had been destroyed in 146 B.C., but according to the historian Pausanias not totally in regard to its public buildings. The new city had been restored by Julius Caesar in 44 B.C., just a hundred years before. The city was then made into a colonia, with duumviri and populated largely with freedmen (cf. 1 Cor. vii. 22) and Jews in great numbers, who had their own synagogue. It had grown rapidly and was now large, prosperous, dissipated[1] and vicious. In the temple of Venus alone, on the summit of the Acropolis, there were as many as a thousand sacred prostitutes.

Corinth, built on the narrow isthmus, had the advantage of both seas and acted as a bridge between the trade of the Aegean and Adriatic. A road of a few miles led up from the port of Cenchreae on the East, and the suburbs of the city must have reached on the other side of the isthmus to the port for the vast cosmopolitan metropolis of Imperial Rome. Corinth herself had a large cosmopolitan population. Moreover, being an obvious emporium for the exchange of trade she grew rapidly, just as Shanghai grew up as an emporium for the exchange of goods between East and West—a huge commercial junction. Corinth was also the administrative capital of Achaia, practically co-extensive with modern Greece, apart from Macedonia. At the time when St. Paul wrote Achaia had become important enough

---

[1] Cf. the Greek proverb referring to the expense of a self-indulgent life at Corinth—οὐ παντὸς ἀνδρὸς ἐς Κόρινθόν ἐσθ᾽ ὁ πλοῦς.

to rank as a senatorial province, and St. Luke's accuracy is to be noted in this connexion. In Acts xviii. 12 he speaks of Gallio, brother of the great Seneca, as being 'proconsul' (ἀνθυπατεύοντος) of Achaia. We know that Achaia had lost its senatorial position under a proconsul in A.D. 15. But in A.D. 44, only a few years before St. Paul paid his first visit, it had been restored. At the time, therefore, when he had first gone there, and at the time when he was writing, Corinth was not only a great centre of commerce but also the seat of government for the whole of Achaia, and administered directly by a proconsul from Rome.

V
Retrospect: St. Paul's First Visit

Let us now take a retrospect, and consider St. Paul's first visit to Corinth.

Considering the character and position of the city it is evident that Corinth must have been a strategic point of the first importance in the spread of the Gospel in the Roman Empire. Whether this had been consciously present in the mind of the great Apostle when he first went there we have no means of ascertaining. But Sir William Ramsay's words are significant. 'According to our view,' he says, 'the residence at Corinth was an epoch in Paul's life. As regards his doctrine he became more clearly conscious of its character, as well as more precise and definite in his presentation of it; and as regards practical work he became more clear as to his aim and the means of attaining the aim, namely that Christianity should be spread through the civilised world, using the freedom of speech which the Imperial policy as declared by Gallio (Acts xviii. 12-17) seemed inclined to permit'.[1] Granting this to be true we may imagine that St. Paul's conception of the importance of Corinth had gradually crystallized in his mind as he continued his work there, and not least through the peculiar difficulties he had to face. These are revealed in outward form in the Acts and in inward essence in the two Epistles to the Corinthians. Let us then look back from the time that the Second Epistle was written in Macedonia, and see what we can learn regarding St. Paul's first visit and the church which

[1] Ramsay *St. Paul the Traveller and Roman Citizen*, p. 260.

he had founded at Corinth some six years earlier. Paul first saw Corinth on his departure from Athens towards the end of his second missionary journey.[1] The date was probably 51 or 52 A.D. He was the 'Father' of the Corinthian Church as he repeatedly makes clear and implies in both his Epistles,[2] and his known helpers were Silas and Timothy.[3] The work was developed later through the agency of Apollos.[4] Peter may also have assisted at Corinth, perhaps more than once while travelling through on his way to or from Rome.[5] Shortly after St. Paul's original arrival at Corinth he had been joined by Silas and Timothy from Macedonia, and his outspoken witness seems to have raised a storm of blasphemous opposition—surely none other than the great adversary's desperate attempt to dislodge him from this strategic centre at the outset of his ministry. But the work was carried on in another house 'hard by the synagogue', a move which, however, can only have reduced the friction in a small degree. Although Crispus, ruler of the synagogue, believed with other Corinthians and was baptized, it seems as though St. Paul was passing on elsewhere. His Master then appeared to him in a vision by night. 'Be not afraid, but speak and hold not thy peace: for I am with thee, and no man shall set on thee to harm thee: for I have much people in this city'. So he continued another eighteen months, gaining converts and establishing the church in the teeth of bitter opposition. Another example of this is seen in his arraignment by the Jews before Gallio, but the proconsul's indifference enabled him to continue, and 'after this he tarried yet many days'.

VI

Internal Conditions

The internal condition of the church now engages our attention. As we have already seen the main facts in connexion with St.

---

[1] Cf. Acts xviii. 1f.
[2] Cf. 1 Cor. iii. 6, 10; iv. 15; ix. 2. 2 Cor. xi. 2; xii. 14.
[3] 2 Cor. i. 19.
[4] Acts xviii. 24-28; 1 Cor. iii. 6.
[5] Dionysius, Bishop of Corinth (c. 170 A.D.) says, 'For both of these (Peter and Paul) having planted us at Corinth, likewise instructed us; and having in like manner taught in Italy they suffered about the same time'. Eusebius, *Ecclesiastical History*, Bk. ii, ch. xxv. Cf. 1 Cor. i. 12.

Paul's first visit to Corinth are to be found in the eighteenth chapter of Acts. From the two extant epistles which he later wrote we may glean further inside information. Paul himself only baptized a few of the converts and adds to the name of Crispus those of Gaius and Stephanas, with his household (1 Cor. i. 14, 16). Crispus was ruler of the synagogue, but the converts as a whole were mainly poor (1 Cor. i. 27). St. Paul lived amongst them working for his own bread. His style was not elaborate. He was 'down in the dust' ($\tau\alpha\pi\epsilon\iota\nu\delta s$) amongst them, his presence 'weak' ($\dot{\alpha}\sigma\theta\epsilon\nu\dot{\eta}s$) and his utterance 'despicable' ($\dot{\epsilon}\xi o\upsilon\theta\epsilon\nu\eta\mu\dot{\epsilon}\nu os$) (2 Cor. x. 1, 10). He was 'determined not to know any thing among them save Jesus Christ and Him crucified', so that the Cross was the sole weapon of his evangelism (1 Cor. ii. 2). At the same time his ministry was marked with special gifts of The Spirit, with 'tongues' (1 Cor. xiv. 18), and with 'mighty signs' (2 Cor. xii. 12), all calculated to penetrate the moral darkness and ignorance of this great city—an instructive phenomenon. The converts were on the whole elementary (1 Cor. iii. 1-4), and the recipients of abnormal gifts of the Holy Spirit, like the Galatians.[1] Deriving in part, perhaps, from the cosmopolitan setting, a markedly independent democratic spirit was present in the church, which led before long to schisms of a more or less personal kind, with a strong tendency to opposition of St. Paul. Spiritual self-conceit was therefore strong, and they were inclined to attach themselves to leading personalities such as Apollos and Cephas. The party which later labelled themselves as Christ's party ($o\dot{\iota}\ X\rho\iota\sigma\tauo\hat{\upsilon}$) (1 Cor. i. 12) were a sect within the Church, probably claiming to give the right account, an almost Ebionite one, of the Messiah. The rapid development of a Judaistic spirit in the Church is what one would expect in a city such as Corinth so largely populated with Jews, not only from Rome but also, no doubt, from other parts of the Roman Empire. In all this we can see that, at Corinth, Church system and discipline were as yet too feeble to control those personal irregularities which, then as now, seem so often to hover in the wake of a true and independent work of The Spirit.

---

[1] Cf. Gal. iii. 5. Such gifts ($\chi\alpha\rho\dot{\iota}\sigma\mu\alpha\tau\alpha$) are not referred to anywhere in the Epistles to the Romans, Ephesians, Philippians, or Colossians.

VII

Further Connexions

In tracing St. Paul's further connexions with Corinth we must deal next with his movements and with his correspondence.

The tendencies which we have just described only began to develop 'a good while' (cf. Acts xviii. 18-23) after the scene before Gallio and after St. Paul had set sail from the port of Cenchreae on the Aegean. From there he went to Ephesus, where he left Aquila and Priscilla, and then went on to Judaea, first going up to Jerusalem and then down to Antioch, the great centre of the Gentile church on the Orontes. From there he set out yet again on his third missionary journey through Galatia and Phrygia, encouraging and strengthening the churches, and making his way eventually by the mainland to Ephesus. In Ephesus he stayed and worked for three whole years (Acts xix). It was during this period that he re-established his connexion with the Corinthian church and wrote his first Epistle.

Intercourse between Ephesus and Corinth was quite free across the sea, and regular by the overland route. Before St. Paul arrived at Ephesus his friends, Aquila and Priscilla, had found Apollos, instructed him in the Christian way and sent him on to Corinth with letters of commendation (Acts xviii. 24-28). Some time after he had been teaching in Corinth and some time after St. Paul had been working in Ephesus news was brought of happenings in the church at Corinth. Certain members of the house of Chloe brought news of 'contentions' (1 Cor. i. 11). The coming of Stephanas and Fortunatus and Achaicus reassured him of their goodwill (1 Cor. xvi. 17).

There are clear indications also of correspondence. St. Paul evidently dealt in a preliminary way with sexual matters in a first letter which is no longer extant.[1] 'I wrote unto you in my

---

[1] Non est dubium quin Petrus et Paulus multa quae hodie non extant scripserint (**There is no doubt that Peter and Paul wrote many things which today are not extant**). (Bengel). 'Many have dropped out of existence. There survive for us as many letters as the providence of the Lord deemed sufficient' (Calvin on 1 Corinthians). See also Lightfoot, *Philippians*, p. 138 and *Notes on the Epistles*, p. 207.

epistle', he said, 'to have no company with fornicators' (1 Cor. v. 9). This letter was written before the First Epistle to the Corinthians and perhaps dispatched direct by sea. The First Epistle itself was then written to deal fully and comprehensively with the same matters. We have as well an indication of yet another epistle, also no longer extant, probably referred to in the second Canonical Epistle (2 Cor. ii. 3, 9, q.v.). This would come between the first and second canonical Epistles, and it may have occasioned the charge against St. Paul that he wavered in his statements between 'Yes' and 'No' (2 Cor. i. 17).

VIII

Setting of the Epistles

We may now deal with the setting of the two Canonical Epistles.

In addition to the visits of Christian friends from Corinth, and the correspondence which St. Paul carried on with the church there, it is quite possible that the apostle himself paid a visit in person. This is, indeed, a view which is held as probable by some.[1] But this visit cannot be asserted as proved, and we therefore prefer to set out as clearly as possible what is actually known from the two Canonical Epistles. These known facts may be formulated as follows:

(a) The first Canonical Epistle, probably written from Ephesus early in 57 A.D., was occasioned by one or two personal visits from Corinthian Christians (1 Cor. i. 11 and xvi. 17). Questions had been submitted relating to a variety of problems. These St. Paul dealt with in his great epistle, together with other allied matters, leading up to his restatement of the essence of his gospel and to his reasoned argument concerning the Resurrection (ch. xv). The whole Epistle also reveals in detail how far the tendencies to which we have referred had developed since St. Paul had founded the church—namely, party spirit and ignorant individualism, unchecked by church government or discipline.

(b) The conditions under which this first Epistle was sent may be seen in its concluding chapter. Reference is there made

---

[1] For a discussion of this see Appendix D.1.

to the collection for the saints destined for Jerusalem (xvi. 1-4). The letter was carried by Titus, with whom Timothy was cooperating (xvi. 10-11). St. Paul announced an impending visit by himself by way of Macedonia (xvi. 5f.). This visit involved a change of plan, as St. Paul had previously indicated that he would go direct to Corinth and from there to Macedonia, returning yet again to Corinth before setting sail a second time from Cenchreae for Judaea (2 Cor. i. 15, 16). But when he made this alteration must remain a chronological puzzle.[1]

(c) Following the dispatch of the first letter St. Paul departed from Roman Asia, bound for Macedonia. This departure was accompanied by a tremendous 'trouble' of some kind, in which he describes himself as 'pressed out of measure, above strength, insomuch that we despaired even of life: we had the sentence of death in ourselves' (2 Cor. i. 8, 9). Various suggestions have been made as to what this terrible ordeal was, but the context leads us to think of bodily illness as well as of perils and anxieties.

We may note that St. Paul's deliverance out of this was for him a veritable resurrection through trust in God 'which raiseth the dead: who delivered us from so great a death, and doth deliver' (2 Cor. i. 9, 10).[2] Moreover, this remarkable experience gave immeasurable power to the comfort which he was able to impart to those to whom he wrote, and seems to colour the whole range of thought of the Epistle. As has been well said, the word 'comfort' (2 Cor. i. 3) 'is pre-eminently characteristic of this Epistle, in which it occurs twelve, or, with the cognate verb, twenty-eight times'.[3]

(d) The general course of St. Paul's movements in leaving Asia is fairly clear. From Ephesus he went to the Troad, hoping to meet Titus, and from thence to Macedonia (Acts xx. 1-3). Meanwhile Titus had not been inactive. As Ramsay points out, he is not mentioned in the First Epistle to the Corinthians 'because he carried that letter'. But his movements and those of his colleagues are referred to in the pasage 2 Corinthians viii. 16f. St. Paul says of Titus that 'he went unto you', and that now he

---

[1] For the change of plan see Appendix D.2.
[2] See below footnote *in loc.* (i. 9). Also Appendix D.3.
[3] E. A. Plumptre in *Ellicott's Commentary* on 2 Cor. i. 3.

was sending him again with a 'brother', and yet another 'brother'. Titus, therefore, had visited Corinth, and had met with success in influencing the brethren, and also in the matter of the λογία or collection. He then met St. Paul in Macedonia and was now ready to bear the Second Epistle.

IX

Writing of the Epistle

The writing of the Second Epistle to the Corinthians arises out of the circumstances which we have just described. We may picture the Apostle composing it, perhaps as we have already suggested in sections, as he travels along the Roman road from one church centre in Macedonia to another in the summer and autumn of the year 57 A.D. The letter which he dictates discloses a state of affairs in Corinth which may be given as follows. In certain respects the situation has improved, and this, of course, brings relief to his spirit. The party feeling is much less complex, and there has been a considerable reaction of loyalty on his behalf. Whereas he describes his feelings before the arrival of Titus with the words 'our flesh had no relief', he is able to express his present experience as not a little 'comforted by the presence of Titus' who had told him of their 'earnest desire', 'mourning', and 'fervent mind' towards him (2 Cor. vii. 7). Moreover there was warm 'zeal' and wholehearted support in the matter of the collection, which had 'provoked very many' in Macedonia to follow their example—probably within the past few months (2 Cor. ix. 2).

All this the Apostle sees is to the good, and it helps him to compose his letter. But at the same time there are present to his mind's eye certain features which indicate deterioration. These must be faced in a spirit of absolute realism and some of them countered with the full weight of his apostolic authority before he finally brings his letter to a close. For one thing the obstinate struggle of immorality to get the upper hand persists. He must

---

[1] καπηλεύω—I hawk, trade in, deal in for purposes of gain. (Souter's Lexicon).

urge them not to be 'unequally yoked with unbelievers: for what fellowship hath righteousness with unrighteousness . . . and what concord hath Christ with Belial?' (2 Cor. vi. 14). But above all he knows that there is a strong and resolute personal opposition to himself. The people he has in mind were quite capable of twisting the motive for his change of plans in a suggestive innuendo of fickleness of purpose (i. 17). At bottom they were 'making merchandise of the Word of God' and therefore incapable of true sincerity (ii. 17).[1] The letters of commendation which they had procured for themselves, perhaps from Pharisaic Christians elsewhere, were writ large in letters of the flesh and meant nothing at all in the way of true spiritual power (iii. 1f.).

These people he will deal with before he closes his Epistle, and, in the interest of the Gospel, with merciless spiritual criticism and exposure. They accused him of walking according to the flesh (x. 2). He will challenge them to stand side by side with him in the matter of allegiance to Christ (x. 7). They were saying that his bodily presence was weak. He will dare them to meet him when he comes (x. 10f.). It is not a question of personalities, but of apostolic principles. The spirit and teaching of these people has nothing at all to do with the spirit of Jesus (xi. 4). They pose as supreme apostles (xi. 5). He will expose them as 'false Apostles, deceitful workers, fashioning themselves into Apostles of Christ' (xi. 13). Yet the issue is also fundamentally a question of character as well as of standing. He will therefore deal with them in a personal manner, and stop their mouths. Arrogance is their patent hall-mark (xi. 20). Service and suffering are the indisputable brands of Christ which mark his life and labours (xi. 21f.).

Thus the letter is written, concluded with tender personal appeals and in the richest vein of grace, and dispatched—to be followed up by a personal visit of 'three months'' duration. During this he was able to compose in a measured manner his great doctrinal treatise to the Romans, which is a fair proof of surrounding peace. Evidently the Epistle dispatched from Macedonia attained its purpose.

PRAYER

A PRAYER OF
KING EDWARD VI

O gracious God and most merciful Father, who hast vouchsafed to us the rich and precious jewel of Thy Holy Word; assist us with Thy Spirit, that it may be written in our hearts to our everlasting comfort; to reform us, to renew us according to Thine own image, to build us up and edify us into the perfect building of Thy Christ, sanctifying and increasing in us all heavenly virtues. Grant this, O heavenly Father, for Jesus Christ's sake.

—AMEN.

Contents

Chapter i

THE POWER OF THE DIVINE παράκλησις IN ACUTE TRIAL

2 Corinthians i. 1-11

To those 'called to be saints' in Corinth this letter would first be read aloud. Perhaps in the house of Justus (Acts xviii. 7), perhaps elsewhere in some large room furnished by a leading disciple, the reader gave to the listening throng of saints, sentence by sentence, uttered for that first time in ears representing universal Christendom, this glorious oracle of God through His chosen vessel. Can we not almost see the scene, and catch the accent and the cadence, and watch the audience—perhaps the very large audience—with their eager faces, as that scroll is opened and, column by column, poured into their ears and hearts?

Let us take our seat beside them, for we are of the same family, and let us listen, too, as those who have never heard before.

Ver. 1. **Paul an apostle of Christ Jesus,** His commissioned representative-messenger,[1] **through God's will,** and therefore commissioned by nothing less than His *fiat,* **and Timotheus the brother,** the fellow-Christian and fellow-worker known to all,[2] **to the Church of God**[3]—the Community of Christians who enjoy the prerogatives of

---

[1] The word ἀπόστολος signifies an ἄγγελος, or messenger, who has in addition a representative character. There is no evidence that 12 was only or always to be the number, except in Rev. xxi. 14, which is mystic, and no wise contrary to the Pauline usage. Barnabas, Silas, James, Andronicus, and Junias are all termed apostles, yet none had 'seen the Lord'.

[2] So we paraphrase ὁ ἀδελφός, the words used likewise of Sosthenes (I Cor. i. 1), and Apollos (I Cor. xvi. 12), and also a little later of Quartus (Rom. xvi. 23). Every Christian is an ἀδελφός among brethren; but ὁ ἀδελφός seems to indicate something *par excellence.* It is used again of Timothy in Col. i. 1.

[3] This is the term used in I and II Thessalonians, I and II Corinthians, and Galatians. The ἐκκλησία is not named in Romans, Philippians, Ephesians, Colossians, 1 Peter, Jude. The phrase 'The Church *of* Ephesus' or 'The Church *of* Corinth,' etc., is never used. See also Hort, *The Christian Ecclesia,* p. 108.

God's ancient Ecclesia in Israel—**which is** even **in Corinth,** and finds
there its own local expression and unity as a representative member of
the great whole, together **with all the holy ones who are** to be found,
in different places and under differing circumstances, **in the whole**
Ver. 2.   province **of Achaia: Grace to you and peace,** free and
benignant divine favour, and its fair resultants of reconciliation
with the Holy One, and inward rest through His presence in the heart,
from God our Father—that Name of infinite nearness and love,
revealed to us in the beloved Son, who has made us His own brethren—
and from the **Lord Jesus Christ**—known *within living memory*, as
dwelling with men in Palestinian villages and towns, spending human
life and dying human death in uttermost literal experience, yet now, in
the Spirit's power, marvellously resident in the Church of God with an
eternal and transcendent glory which cannot be hid.

Such is the salutation, and perhaps the reader pauses for a
moment in the Christian assembly while his audience reflect on
the presence of The Lord Himself in their midst, and recollect
the well-known face of the great Apostle who has sent the letter
and will soon be with them. Let us listen to his message:

Ver. 3.   **Blessed,** praised with worshipping love, be **the God and**
Father of our Lord Jesus Christ; HE 'who inhabiteth eternity', 'dwelling in the light unapproachable', unknown and unknowable
in His 'perfection', but knowable and known, and near, and dear in *this*
respect, that our risen Lord called Him, in human hearing (John **xx.** 17),
'My Father and your Father, my God and your God'; **the Father of**
Divine **mercies,** in the special form of cheer from above under suffering
in Christ's cause, and **God of all encouragement,** the tender cheer
and comfort which love can give to a beloved one by meeting his inmost
Ver. 4.   need,[1] **who encourages us** with renewed and repeated cheer
each time **in all** the experiences of **our tribulation** and
suffering; and this He does **in order to enable us,** empowered within,
to pass it on to others, and in our turn **to encourage those** who are
in all manner of **tribulation,** and to do it **by means of that** very
encouragement, that cheer from above, **whereby we ourselves are**
sensibly **encouraged**[2] **by** none other than **God Himself. For, just**
Ver. 5.   as there **overflow to us**[3] **the sufferings**, which we experience
on account of our union with Christ and our devotion to the

---

[1] Ecce Deus Noster! (**Behold our God!**).
[2] Sequentia sancta. (**Holy sequence**).
[3] I Pet. i. 11. εἰς Χριστὸν

2

service of Christ, so that we sometimes feel we have more than we can contain, and find that we have more than we can endure; so in like manner through Christ, who is the channel of all bounty and blessing, there overflows also our encouragement, for again we have more than we can contain, and there are other vessels to be filled likewise

Ver. 6.   with cheer from on high. But (δὲ) it makes no difference as regards blessing to you, for whether we are afflicted in undergoing these experiences, which press us down to the very grave and gate of death, it is with a view to your encouragement, in bringing you renewal of spiritual life, and for your salvation, that you may enjoy spiritual safety, health, and joy in your renewed experience of God's grace: whether on the other hand we ourselves are encouraged through renewal of life-giving grace, still it is for your encouragement —an encouragement which, through the God-given infection of our cheer, energizes you in the experience of a persistent endurance of the same sufferings, i.e. in the same family, and therefore inseparable from those which we also suffer, and which are indeed the very gateway

Ver. 7.   of blessing and of God-given cheer.[1] And our hope and confident expectation for you, as to the eventual issue of all these varied experiences is perfectly secure, knowing assuredly that as you are fellow sharers of the sufferings on Christ's behalf and for His Name's sake, so also are you assuredly of the encouragement, which lifts us up and carries us on.

The Apostle is resolved at the outset to lay bare his own heart, and to speak, in some detail at least, of his own recent experience.

Ver. 8.   Now this emphasis on God's comfort, and our sufferings and consolations, and His power within us, is not without pointed and personal reference, for I would not have you ignorant brethren, rather do I delight in confidence and information on matters which affect us both, and indeed I am sure you are aware of the recent tribulation and terrible crisis of ours which overtook us in Asia;[2] that overwhelmingly and in a manner altogether beyond our strength, we were burthened and borne right down, insomuch that we despaired

Ver. 9.   even of life, feeling in our collapse of health that the end had come: but to our queries concerning recovery we had in ourselves the answer of death (τοῦ θανάτου)—'death', indeed we felt, and can still feel (ἐσχήκαμεν) that answer to every question ringing in our

---

[1] Ver. 6. Animus absolutè pastoralis! (The shepherd's heart completely!).
[2] Occasione prorsus ignota (On an occasion quite unknown). See Appendix D.2.

ears, **in order that,** although we even said, 'We shall die', yet actually
we should not put our **trust in ourselves, but** rather be driven to
Ver. 10.   trust **in God who raises the dead.**[1] He it was, God Himself,
      Who rescued us out of so great a death—and is still
rescuing us (read *ῥύεται*) under whatever remains of the trial, so that its
after-affects become fainter and fainter—**in Whom we hope,** continuing
Ver. 11.   in our reliance on Him, **that He will yet** again and again
      rescue us, **you also co-operating** in a subordinate capacity,
in putting your shoulders under the burden **in** united **prayer on our
behalf; so that through** our **many intercessors** (*προσώπων*) **the** gracious
gift of God to us, in answer to those prayers, and in deliverance from
danger and suffering, correspondingly **by many, may be received
with thanks,** being recognized as God's gracious goodness through
them, **on our behalf.**

We have finished our paraphrase of the first section of the
Epistle. Let us stand back to gain a better view of these two
figures—the Apostle Paul who dictates his name at the head of
the Epistle, and the Lord of Comfort who diffuses all that is
written with the glory of His grace.

To the letter-writer of that day it was as much a matter of
course to prefix the personal name to the letter as it is to us to
append it. But then, as now, the name was not a mere word of
routine; certainly not in the communications of a religious
leader. It avowed responsibility; it put in evidence a person.
And where in Holy Scripture do we come closer to this eager and
wonderful personality than in this Epistle, and who of all the
saints of the Bible, is more the living man to us than this Paul?
Reading this Second Epistle to the Corinthians we feel as if we
can see his face, and touch his hand, and catch the accent of his
voice, and detect the tears in his tired eyes. We come to feel that
we know him in his splendid strength; the strength of nature,
shown in an intellect, a will, a love, an anger, yes, a righteous

---

[1] See *Memoir and Remains of the Revd. Robert Murray McCheyne,* by Dr.
A. Bonar, for a remarkable historical parallel to the experience of St. Paul.
McCheyne, in 1839, in a veritable resurrection, was delivered from death at
Bouja, near Smyrna, in modern Asia Minor, at the same time as his flock
experienced revival at St. Peter's, Dundee. *Memoir,* ch. iv. (Ed.).

indignation, of the highest kind; above all, the strength of grace, 'the power of Christ overarching him' (xii. 9), 'Christ magnified in his body' (Phil. i. 20), so that indeed, the LORD looked from his eyes, spoke from his lips, moved and acted in his behaviour; 'not he, but Christ' (Gal. ii. 20). Such is Paul the Apostle who sends this Epistle.

As he begins the Apostle reminds us all is of GOD, whose name is blessed as 'the Father of mercies' and 'the God of all comfort'. Then 'from God' there steps out, as it were, The Lord Jesus Christ, 'The Lord of mercies' and 'The Lord of all comfort'. Let us look to Him and allow our hearts to find rest in the contemplation of His person. A careful reading of the text will make it clear that in this passage we are not encouraged to think directly of the redeeming virtue of the crucified Lord. Rather, we are looking on Him as wonderfully fitted, by the unknown as well as the known sufferings of His sacrifice, to be CHRISTUS CONSOLATOR. Strong in His personal love and willingness, rich with His unspeakably personal experience, He is able to 'be touched with the feeling of our infirmities' (Heb. iv. 15) and our wounds. He is 'able to save, to the uttermost' (Heb. vii. 25), from all their weariness and their heavy loads, those who will let Him have His way. He is able, with personal methods of His own, to transfigure sorrows into joys. Consider HIM. Let it sink always deeper into our torn and tired spirits that such a Person exists, that *this* Person exists—living, loving, accessible. He is indeed 'the Man at the Gate' whom readers of *Pilgrim's Progress* will remember. 'Here is a poor burthened sinner', said the Pilgrim; 'I would know, Sir, if you are willing to let me in'. 'Here,' let us say, 'are stricken and broken hearts; we have heard, Sir, that your heart was once broken, and has stood open ever since, and that its great rift is turned into a gate by which men go in and find peace. We would know if you are willing to let us in'.

'I am willing with all my heart,' said the Man; and with that he opened the gate.

5

Chapter ii

A DIGRESSION CONCERNING THE LORD—CHRIST THE 'YEA' AND THE 'AMEN' OF PROMISE

2 Corinthians i. 12-22

WE have seen how St. Paul, at the end of the opening passage of his Epistle, reckons on the sympathetic support of many in prayer, and on their thanksgiving for his deliverance. He will now have to begin to deal with some of his critics. But, if there is one thing of which he is sure and proud, it is of complete loyalty to God as His minister, and particularly in his unreserved devotion to them. So he proceeds:

Ver. 12. **For our rejoicing,** the happiness of our inward certainty, **is this,** even **the witness of our conscience**[1] which tells us, malign us who will, **that in holy simplicity** of purpose and a **sincerity** examined in the light **of God** and found pure, **not in fleshly wisdom** of human design or scheme **but in God's grace, we have behaved in the world**[2] (ἐν τῷ κόσμῳ)[3] and **specially towards you. For we** Ver. 13. **are not writing to you** and expressing in this letter **anything but just what you** can **read,** and see in your hands already expressed in previous letters, **and what you** cannot but **understand** by looking at it, **and will I trust** have reason to **understand** even **to the close** of the whole matter, **as you have in fact** (καὶ) **understood us to some** Ver. 14. **extent** (ἀπὸ μέρους), imperfect as your insight of our principle has been; and I trust that you will come to see what the purport of all is, **that you are our joy** and cause for pride, **even as** we believe **we are yours in** prospect of **the Day of** the Return of **our Lord Jesus** (cf. I Thess. ii. 19, 20) that Day of Blessed Hope when we shall all know The Lord and each other, even as we are known.

---

[1] ἐν πνεύματι. Rom. ix. 1.
[2] Totam vitam prolepticè summat more Domini (**He gathers up proleptically the whole of his life, in the manner of the Lord**) (John xvii. 6).
[3] ἐν τῷ κόσμῳ may here signify 'in practical life'.

He will now deal with one of the causes of friction and mis-understanding between himself and some in Corinth. This was due to his change of plans. He knew, indeed, that his change of travelling plan had been misunderstood, as if his delay in a promised visit meant a certain alienation. But no. It was not so. He had been prompted from the start by confiding affection for them.

Ver. 15. **And** further, **in this confidence** in your understanding of how matters lay, **I proposed,** on leaving Ephesus, **to come straight** over **to you** before any other tour, **so that you might have a second benefit** (in the early opportunity of a development of grace Ver. 16. through my presence with you again), **and by** taking **you** 'en route' **to pass on into Macedonia, and then again from Macedonia to pass** back **to you** 'en route' for Jerusalem, **and** thus Ver. 17. **by you,** and with your God-speed, **to be sped forward** on my way **on to Judaea. When therefore I was proposing this,** and indeed cherishing this intention, **did I behave with capriciousness?**[1] Do you really think that could be? **Or the things** which **I** purpose and **propose** in my planning **do I propose** them **'flesh-wise',** and therefore at the dictates of self, **so that** there should ever be **in 'my' hands,** rather than in His, **the** decisive **'Yes, Yes'** or **the** decisive **'No, No',** to shift about as I happen to like myself?

At this point St. Paul begins his digression.[2]

Ver. 18. **But,** by way of contrast to this uncertainty of behaviour, and **God is** a **faithful** witness to it, **our word to you,** whether in preaching, writing, or personal intercourse, **is not** a 'Yes-word' **and** then, mixed in with it, a 'No-word'. **For** everything is determined by Ver. 19. the great personal object of our faith, even **our** ($\tau o \hat{\upsilon}$) **God's Son Christ Jesus; He Who was proclaimed** in Gospel preaching and teaching **amongst you by us—that is by me and Silvanus and Timotheus—was not,** when first you heard, and never at any time was found to be, an alternating or hybrid **'Yes' and 'No', but** much rather, **was** completely proved to be **in Himself** nothing less than Ver. 20. an embodiment of an ever blessed **'Yes'. For every promise of God,** through the whole vast range of Holy Scripture, has

---

[1] Ita nonnulli dixerant! **(So some had said!).** See Appendix D.2.
[2] Digreditur de Domino! **(He digresses concerning the Lord!)** (Vv. 18-22.)

7

in Him and in His person **its** initial **'Yes'** of purpose, **and so** also **through Him its** final **'Verily'** of fulfilment, leading **to our** (τῷ) **God's glory through us** as means, being the messengers of such a Saviour.

'All the promises of God in Him are Yea, and in Him Amen'. So the beautiful and familiar Authorised Version renders it in simple dignity. St. Paul's digression has led him now to this point. He has been speaking about himself, and his missionary plans, and his mode of preaching. But he *cannot help* referring to the Lord. He glides, as if he could not stop his gravitation, from the other subject to Christ. He gladly turns off, and therefore let us also turn aside for a while to speak of the unchangeableness of Christ, and the fixed eternal certainties of His truthful promises. Christ *overflows* everywhere into what Paul says. And in this we have a rich and beautiful illustration of the all importance of Christ, the omnipresence of Christ, in every part of the Gospel, and in every part of His followers' lives.

Let us take a few of the great promises of God, and in them as examples see what is meant by the Yea and Amen in Jesus of all the promises.

1. THE PROMISE OF PARDON to the sinful soul. 'I will love you freely' (Hos. xiv. 4). 'Thou wilt cast all their sins into the bottom of the sea' (Mic. vii. 19). 'Their sins and iniquities will I remember no more' (Heb. x. 17). The very freedom and fulness of this offer of God's forgiveness is that which often makes man doubt and hesitate, sometimes for long and weary years, whether it says what it seems to say; whether it may be accepted without reserve. Is it not clogged with exacting conditions? Must I not be holy before I can be welcomed? Must I not work all my life long before I can be accepted? When we think what acceptance is, and what sin is, we might well wonder thus, if it were not for the Yea and Amen in Jesus Christ. But HE is there to prove that God means not little but much; not reluctant toleration, but abundant mercy. Look at self and you are right in despairing of pardon for *any* sin. Look to the SON of God and your troubled soul may trust the promise of the pardon of *all* sin. Jesus stands

there as the gift of God, Jesus the Son. The invisible pardon becomes in Him, as it were, visible. You may trust it, because the Son of God came, and died, and lives. Let us act in humble simplicity on that Yea and that Amen.

2. THE PROMISES OF HOLINESS, of an inner separation from serving sin, and a reception of divine power and purity in the heart. Here, indeed, the promise, in many varying forms, is magnificently full. 'These things write I unto you, that ye sin not' (1 John ii. 1). 'Whosoever abideth in Him sinneth not' (1 John iii. 6). 'Let not sin reign in your mortal body' (Rom. vi. 12). 'As He which hath called you is holy, so be ye holy in all manner of conduct' (1 Peter i. 15). How can all this possibly be?

> 'Ah, how can this unready will
> At once, at every point, repel
> The heart's own traitors, aided still
> By energies of hell?'

It is impossible apart from Him but wonderfully possible 'in Him', who is at once the Yea of the promise, and the Amen of its fulfilment. The secret is not it, but He Himself. 'Christ is made unto us sanctification' (1 Cor. i. 30). 'Ye are filled full in Him' (Col. ii. 10). 'That Christ may dwell in your hearts, by faith; that ye may know the love of Christ, which passeth knowledge' (Eph. iii. 17, 19).

3. Next, and lastly, take THE PROMISE OF HEAVEN. 'He hath prepared for them a city' (Heb. xi. 16). 'They seek a heavenly country' (Heb. xi. 14). 'Our conversation is in heaven' (Phil. iii. 20). 'We shall ever be with The Lord' (1 Thess. iv. 17). Oh, wonderful promise!

> 'Thrice blessed, bliss-inspiring hope,
> It lifts the fainting spirit up,
> It brings to life the dead'.

Dear, holy hope! It is the light of the dying Christian's soul; it is the light of the Christian mourner's soul, in the midnight and desolation of a great bereavement. A life beyond death for ever; an indestructible home of holiness and joy, far off, and yet so near.

Yes; and how do we know it? Can we see, can we reach, can
we touch it? Even if we could, could we be sure that it is for *us*,
for any but the greatest saints and sufferers? Could anything
but a martyr's life and death purchase such an eternity? There
are ten thousand difficulties, apart from Christ. The question
of the very existence of heaven, apart from Him, would be to us
but a riddle and a dream. But in Him the promise is Yea and
Amen, to every one that believeth. He has died; He has risen;
He has shown Himself alive; He has gone up thither; He has
promised to return and take to Himself there the youngest,
feeblest soul that believes on Him. 'When THOU didst overcome
the sharpness of death, Thou didst open the Kingdom of heaven
to all believers'. Thou didst let the light in on the Kingdom.
Thou didst open the gate into the Kingdom. Heaven is a smaller
gift than Thou, Lord Jesus Christ. He who gave Thee to the
sinner will not refuse the city.

So it is with *all* the promises. They are not words only, they
are facts, in the Lord Jesus Christ. St. Paul returns to speak
of our 'possession' of the promises (vii. 1) when we shall meditate
again with him on this great subject.[1] In our present passage let
us see how in conclusion he sets the Divine seal of The Spirit
on 'all the promises of God'.

Ver. 21.   **Now He Who secures us** as His legal property **(together
with you)** so that we are embodied **into Christ, and** Who
anointed us, is none other than **God** Himself, **who also sealed us,**
Ver. 22.   ratifying His ownership over us, **and gifted us with The
Spirit's earnest** (ἀρραβών)—a pledge or payment on account of
that complete glory, which now is experienced only in part—inwardly
in our hearts.

These concluding verses describe the inner life of the Christian,
and we can see in them the inward working of the Triune God—
Christ who anointed us, God who sealed us, The Spirit's earnest
in our hearts. As in the concluding words of the whole epistle
(xiii. 14) we may here discern each person of The Blessed Trinity.

---

[1] See below, p. 61-2.

Behold the FATHER, 'God and Father of Our Lord Jesus Christ' —The Father Who is the Fountain of the whole redeeming work; promising, blessing, choosing, accepting, adopting, securing, working all things in the light of His own benignant will. Behold the SON, the Beloved One in His own Baptism and the One in Whom we are incorporated and embodied so that we also are accepted in The Beloved. He lives to be the 'Head' of His people; their Source of life, their Secret of power, their unifying Centre; and the day is coming when that Headship will be seen as the centre of a whole Universe of holy life, the day when inward experience and outward expression will coincide in eternal joy—the day of His return (cf. vv. 14, 15). Look again, and behold the SPIRIT!

> 'Behold Him dwell in all the saints
> And seal the heirs of heaven'.

He comes, the Promise of the Father. Contact, in humblest faith, with Christ and union with Him implies reception of the Spirit, the Lord, the Life-giver, the Sanctifier. He is 'the anointing Spirit'. He is the Pledge, or earnest, the *arrhâbôn*, or part-payment given as promise of the whole against 'the glory to be revealed in us'. Now this is experienced in our hearts, but in the brightness of that day not only 'the sufferings of this present time' but its experiences of grace will so fade in the comparison that it will be as if they had scarcely been at all. 'The purchased possession' of our God will be so emancipated then into the eternal freedom that it will be as if its 'redemption' had but just been achieved.

Great and wonderful are the promises. It is guaranteed for believing sinners that here they shall be, in the Beloved One, the very 'sons of God', walking and pleasing Him. It is sealed and guaranteed for them that hereafter, when their Lord's time shall come, they shall 'appear with Him in glory', such a glory that 'it doth not yet appear what they shall be'. How can these things be? The effect is great; but the CAUSE is greater.

> Of FATHER, SON, and SPIRIT we
> Extol the threefold care,
> Whose love, whose merit, and whose power,
> Unite to lift us there.

Chapter iii

PASTORAL AND MISSIONARY CONCERNS: THE INFINITELY IMPORTANT ISSUES OF RECEPTION OR REJECTION OF THE GOSPEL

2 Corinthians i. 23-ii. 17

THE passage begins with a resumption from Ch. i. ver. 17 of what St. Paul had been saying about his alteration of plans.

Ch. i. 23. **But** this by the way. I return to my change of plan. Why did I not come first to you, but first thus to Macedonia? **I call upon God as witness,** in uttermost solemnity, **upon my soul,** that just **to spare you** pain—it was love for you—**I gave up** (οὐκέτι) **coming to Corinth.** When I say 'spare', I have no thought of dictation. For it is

Ver. 24. **not that we have** any **lordship** in respect **of your faith**— that is a matter completely between your Lord and your own souls, and we do not want to dictate a new creed to you—**but** rather **we are fellow-workers** wishing to co-operate **for your joy**[1] in the one path of joy, holiness; **as for your faith,** in that matter **you stand aright,**[2] and there we have no wish, as we have no need, to dictate.

Ch. ii. 1 **No** (δὲ) **I made up my mind**[3] **to this,** my delay being due to a resolve deep as my heart, **not** to pay you a visit **back** (πάλιν)[4] **in painful grief,** and under such conditions **to come to you** —I could not bear it.

Here the Apostle digresses. He visualizes what would happen if he came to them in grief and pain, and for the purpose of Apostolic discipline. There would inevitably be a scene. Moreover, the disciplinary action towards the offender of whom he had

---

[1] Apostolus non Papa! **(The Apostle, not a Pope!)** cf. 1 Pet. v. 3.
[2] quoad fidem, bene est vobiscum **(as regards your faith, it is well with you.)**
[3] In Domino ipse consulit secum **(He deliberates with himself 'in the Lord.')**
[4] See Appendix D.1.

written (1 Cor. v. 1f.) would mean that person being finally driven out altogether and perhaps irretrievably lost.[1] If, therefore, we wish to understand what is in his mind we need to look on to verse 11, where his concern about these matters eventually stands disclosed, in his reference to the great adversary of whose designs he is not ignorant.[2]

Ver. 2. **For if** once **I grieve you, who then** (καὶ) **is there to gladden me, but the one who has been grieved by me,** seeing I am inconsolable, except by your renewed happiness in each and all;

Ver. 3. **and** in the last letter **I wrote** I had **this very thing** in mind, and I wrote it **in order that on coming I might not have** to suffer **grief from those** very persons **who should** naturally **be my joy,** and **I relied on you all** and on your united sympathy with the thought in my mind, and indeed I took it for granted, **that my joy is the joy of you all,** so that you could not wish me to come for only sorrow.

Ver. 4. **For** it was **out of much tribulation** of spirit **and stress of heart I wrote** that letter **to you,** yes indeed **with a shower of tears** (πολλῶν δακρύων), and I wrote it, **not in order that you might be grieved** and made to suffer, **but that you might know** and have evidence of **the** deep deep **love which I have more abundantly towards you.**[3]

Ver. 5. **But if anyone has caused grief** (and I am thinking of the individual of whom I wrote and what he did did give me great pain)[4] yet after all I know that it is **not me he has grieved,** anyhow, not me only, **but, to some extent (that I may not burden you,** for I must

Ver. 6. not let you carry too much) he has grieved **all of you.** And now what of that case? It has been **enough for the person in question** to have had **this penalty, the** rebuke administered **by the majority** is enough, without the awful sequel which I originally

Ver. 7. announced,[5] **so that** now **on the contrary you** ought **the rather to forgive and cheer** him, and so rescue him, **lest it should happen that the person in question**[6] should **be drowned**

Ver. 8. **with** his **excessive** and therefore killing **grief. Wherefore** in view of that grief **I appeal to you to confirm to him** and

---

[1] Verus pastor! **(True shepherd!).**

[2] Hic incipit pericope digrediens, et ver. 11 explicit **(Here begins a paragraph which digresses, and ver. 11 explains).**

[3] Ver. 4. Verus pastor **(True shepherd).**

[4] He is passing on to speak 'De peccatore iam paenitenti restaurando' **(Concerning the restoration of a sinner now a penitent).**

[5] 1 Cor. v. 5.

[6] revera paenitens **(really penitent).**

make him feel your **love, for for this purpose also I wrote** my original

Ver. 9.   message[1] calling for extreme discipline, not for a mere mechanical execution but **that I might know your approved character, as to your being obedient in everything** and entirely

Ver. 10.   loyal. **But to whom you forgive anything, I also** forgive it, so that your pardon will now carry mine with it; **for indeed** (καὶ) **what I have forgiven (so far as I have any need to grant forgiveness** (εἴ τι κεχάρισμαι)) **is wholly in your interest** (δι' ὑμᾶς) not mine,

Ver. 11.   it is **in the Lord's presence,** and it is **in order that we should not be defrauded by Satan,**[2] thus thwarting the Enemy, **for we are not without cognizance of his designs,** knowing very well his plans, and that he would gladly rob us of a brother through despair.

The verses we have just paraphrased form part of the wonderful discourse concerning the trials, toils, strength, and glory, of Ministry for Christ, which occupies the opening chapters of this great Epistle. In all this nothing is said about the exterior of the thing, about gradations and subordinations of rank, about divisions of labour and of honour. Everything is said about the spiritual relations of the minister to the Lord, and to the flock, and to the Gospel, and to himself. We may consider, therefore, at this point two suggestive spiritual themes, which are found in these verses— *The Reality of the Adversary*, who is the thief, and *The Precious Treasure of the Church*, which is Christian happiness and unity.

'An enemy hath done this' (Matt. xiii. 28). So the master of the field, in our Lord's parable, said to his servants. The parable was told by Our Lord Himself and, when we ponder the nature of this enemy with the whole of the fourfold Gospel before us, we realize beyond all question the Evil One was a tremendous reality to the Holy One Himself, and to the teachers which He trained and inspired. Not *it* but *he* assailed Him with all the subtlety of allurement in the desert (Luke iv. 6). Not *it* but *he* spoke to the Christ a deadly suggestion through the lips of Peter (Matt. xvi. 22, 23). Not *it* but *he* was permitted to put the

---

[1] Or perhaps just—'recent written message', i.e. in the letter between **the** two canonical epistles.
[2] Ne Satanas ovem auferat (**Lest Satan should carry off a sheep**).

Apostles to fiery tests (Luke xxii. 3, 31), to possess one of them fully and finally, and to drag another into the great denial.

It was not otherwise with St. Paul. He knew from a wide and varied experience that he had a personal enemy of righteousness with whom to contend. He knew how the adversary might destroy the sanctity of Christian married life (1 Cor. vii. 5). He was particularly aware of the deep deceit of some, working within his own plot, who called themselves apostles but were actually agents of the enemy of souls (2 Cor. xi. 13, 14). All the time he carried in his own body 'a thorn in the flesh, the messenger of Satan to buffet him' (2 Cor. xii. 7). In the letter which he was shortly to write to Rome he is aware of the hindering and spoiling work of Satan within the Church, and gives wary advice for the defeat of his objectives (Rom. xvi. 17-20). So here also he meets stratagem with strategy. He urges the restoration of the penitent lest he be overwhelmed with too much grief and so lost. Through personal distress, through plain speech and through spiritual power he seeks both to encourage the happiness of the Church and to retain the individual.

Yes, and the prize was worth contending for, the treasure was worth guarding. It was, indeed, nothing less than that very unity for which The Lord of the Church had Himself prayed—a unity the quality of which was primarily and vitally spiritual and from within. It was not, as His great prayer showed all through (John xvii), to be imposed upon the community from without, but generated within the inner life and derived altogether from above. It was to have regard to the action of the Father and the Son upon the saints; to the dwelling of Christ in the heart, and the dwelling of the heart in Christ by faith. Therefore its immediate outlook in the first place rises above all problems of order, and even of ordinance; it touches immediately the life hid with Christ in God. Moreover it finds expression in a believing community totally different from a mere aggregation, for it at once demands individuality and transcends it; it is a common life of love, love generated by the love of Him Who is, eternally and within Himself, Love.

All this is found likewise in the thought, teaching, and practice of St. Paul. In the first Epistle he had dealt with the principles of the body and its motive power of love. Here in the Second Epistle we see him putting these same principles into practice. All through his appeal is spiritual. He visualises the inner life of the Church where the Lord moves amidst the candlesticks. All is 'in the Lord's presence' (vs. 10). Running through is the appeal to love, the more excellent way (vs. 4 and 8, cf. 1 Cor. xii. 31). His concern is for the body and for the members in particular (1 Cor. xii. 27). Where one member suffers all suffer with it—including himself (v. 5, cf. 1 Cor. xii. 26). There should be no schism, so he appeals for the restoration of the penitent offender (v. 8, cf. 1 Cor. xii. 25). So he earnestly seeks to preserve the harmony of the body and at the same time to consider each member in particular.

The Apostle now returns to his change of plans. But with an altered emphasis—this time introducing his missionary objectives.

Ver. 12. **But** (δέ), oh that I could make you realize my intense thought of you! On leaving Ephesus, on my altered programme, **I reached the Troad,**[1] **with missionary intentions** (εἰς τὸ εὐαγγέλιον) for the Gospel **of Christ,** and **a large opportunity** (θύρας) **presented itself** there for work **as The Lord's agent** (ἐν Κυρίῳ). But I could not take it. It was at Troas that I had expected to meet my brother Titus on his return from seeing you. **I could have** (ἔσχηκα)[2] **no** feeling of **spiritual rest, at my not finding my brother Titus** who had not appeared, **but quitting them** there, my Troad brethren, **I left** at once **for Macedonia.**

Here he digresses again on this theme—that all his itineraries are controlled by Christ alone, and all work out to the glory of Christ.

---

[1] See Appendix D.3 p. 157.
[2] 'The perfect ἔσχηκα seems at first sight out of place, but it is more expressive than the aorist. It suggests the *continuous* expectation of relief, which was always anew disappointed'. (Denney).

The anxiety is over now; we have met; and Titus has told me the good
Ver. 14. news. **So** (δὲ) **thanks be to God, who thus always** (τῷ πάντοτε)
leads us, His soldiers, **in the triumph-procession**[1] **of His
Christ,** from place to place, now by joy now by trial, **and sheds the
odour of the knowledge of Him** in His Gospel **everywhere by our
means. For such a sweet savour are we** indeed **as Christ's**
Ver. 15. (Χριστοῦ), His messengers in His hand **for His Father's purposes** (τῷ Θεῷ), **in the case of those on the road of salvation** (σωζομένοις)
and in the case of those on that of ruin (ἀπολλυμένοις); but alas not
Ver. 16. with like effect on all, **for we to the one** are **an odour breathing death and developing death,** as they hasten their doom
by rejecting the truth, **to the others an odour breathing life and
Ver. 17. quickening** and developing **life.** Mysterious ministry! **And
who can sustain it, unaided from above?** To be a preacher
may seem a light thing to the mercenary and the insincere; it is as awful
as it is dear a charge to *us*. **For we are not like the crowd** of would-be
propagandists, **tamperers**[2] **with the Divine message, but as out of a
single heart, but as sent out by God,** working **before the eyes of God,
in union with Christ** (ἐν Χριστῷ)—thus do **we speak,** such indeed is
the condition of our utterance of the truth.[3]

Here the Apostle gives us the infinitely important issues
involved in the proclamation and reception of the Gospel. Here
let the reader pause, first putting himself in the place of the
listener, and then in the position of the preacher, questioning
himself in the presence of the Lord.

Have I fled for refuge? Am I in Christ? Do I, personally,
accept Him as my Life, my Hope, my Lord? Have I given my
heart to God? Is 'building up' what I want? Or has the very
foundation still to be begun? The trench for it indeed is cut, for
Jesus died, wounded for my transgressions. But is the building
in the trench begun, are the root-stones laid there on the living
rock, by my being drawn to Him?

Ah, let the preacher here solemnly warn you, with some faint
echo of apostolic warnings, that nothing else will do. Out of

---

[1] θριαμβεύοντι—triumphatos circumducenti (**By leading round those who
have been won in victory**).

[2] The derived meaning of καπηλεύοντες, cf. 2 Cor. iv. 2.

[3] V. 17. Lex apostolicae praedicationis (**The law of apostolic proclamation**).

Christ no salvation. 'Neither is there salvation in any other'.
'He that hath not the Son the wrath of God abideth upon him'.
Beware of the house upon the sand; the storm will spare nothing
but what is really founded on the rock. Oh, you that hear but
do not; that approve of Christ but do not love Him; that think
about Him but do not come to Him; or you that doubt Him but
are content to doubt, that will not look your doubts in the face
and bring them to the test of at least the experiment of resolute
Bible-searching and active prayer; oh, brother, who for one cause
or another art lingering on in the suburbs of the City of Destruction; let the preacher in respectful earnest love try not to preach
smooth things, not to make out that you can somehow do without
quite coming to your Lord—but implore you, 'Be ye reconciled
to God'. Escape to the mountain, stay not in the plain. Remember the impending Eternity, and take the one possible refuge—in
the very arms of the Eternal.

The preacher likewise must needs know he is a sinner, saved
by grace, and thus question himself:

> Has He found thy message true?
> Truth, and truly spoken, too?
> Utter'd with a purpose whole
> From a self-forgetful soul,
> Bent on nothing save the fame
> Of the great redeeming Name,
> And the pardon, life and bliss,
> Of the flock He bought for His?
>
> Think!—but, ah, with thoughts like these,
> Hasten, sinner, to thy knees.

Chapter iv

THE CONTENTS AND SUPREME SIGNIFICANCE OF THE NEW COVENANT OF THE SPIRIT

2 Corinthians iii. 1-18

At the end of the previous passage, after Ch. ii. ver. 17, the Apostle pauses, conscious of his critics.

Such an avowal of principle and character, alas, may be misunderstood by some of you. So do not mistake this solemn affirmation of our
Ver. 1.   mission and our motive. In speaking thus **are we beginning** afresh by going **back** (πάλιν), as when we first came, and as if we now felt the need **to substantiate ourselves** in our original claim to your attention? **Surely, we do not need (like certain** other visitors) **substantiating letters to you, or,** to other churches, **from you?** We
Ver. 2.   have such a letter, good everywhere and always. **Our letter—** why **you yourselves are** our letter, you our own true converts and the Lord's seal to our labour. And it is **written,** where? **On our** opened **hearts,** that all may scan our love,[1] and that our letter may be **recognized** (γινωσκομένη) **and,** being recognized, be **read** (ἀναγινωσκομένη) **by all and sundry** (ὑπὸ πάντων ἀνθρώπων). They have but to see what Corinth is to us to know that Corinth is our spiritual child.
Ver. 3.   To such eyes there is no mistaking your significance (**since it is evidently seen in you**) that you are in truth **Christ's own letter, taken down** (διακονηθεῖσα) from Him **by us,** who are thus at once His scribes and His materials or papyrus. It is **inscribed not with ink but with** the Holy Ghost—**Spirit of the God who is eternal life;** the Holy Spirit has filled us with this love for you. It is engraved, **not** like the law **on tablets of stone, but** put with letters of love **on fleshly tablets of the heart.**[2]

The verses we have paraphrased deal with the subject of 'living epistles'—the bright reality of true Christian experience,

---

[1] Sc. omnes legere possunt amorem nostrum erga vos; cor nostrum patet (**All can read our love towards you; our heart lies open**).

[2] Internal reasons strong for καρδίας, unless indeed καρδίαις is an early gloss.

the product of the Gospel. Similar thoughts of Divine origin the Apostle now proceeds to apply to his own ministry of the same Gospel, and is soon dealing with eternal verities, and the New Covenant in particular.

Ver. 4.   Here is **boldness** (πεποίθησιν) indeed; **but** (δὲ) **this we have** without misgiving; for it is possible **through Christ,** and Christ alone, as **before God's very face.** Yes, through Christ alone; **for it is not that we are competent from ourselves**—we Ver. 5.   are utterly incompetent from our inner consciousness, our own natural resources, **to calculate out a Gospel,**[1] delivered **as from self,** a self-originated (ἐξ) message. **No, our competence** and qualification as gospellers **comes from God** alone,[2] and from Him it does come Ver. 6.   **—He,** who, being our converter and inspirer, **did also** thus **give us competence** and actually qualify us as **agents of a New Covenant**[3]—**not Letter but Spirit,** not the edict, 'Do this and Live', but the promise, 'I will pour out my Spirit'. Profound, essential contrast! We cannot mingle or compromise the two in a blessed Gospel: they refuse it by their nature and effect; **the Letter,**[4] the inscribed Edict, **kills,** sentences the transgressor unconditionally to the death of the soul;[5] **the Spirit,**[4] the great Gospel promise and gift, transforming the pardoned into the holy, **makes alive,** enables man to live, in peace, to God.

In these verses we reach the very heart of the chapter. St. Paul has lost little time in reaching this point. Let us make a break here to give a little more detailed consideration to what he has said.

'We are not sufficient of ourselves to think anything as of ourselves' is the familiar rendering of the Authorized Version. We might say 'to reason out anything, as from ourselves'. But it is evident that in so speaking he does not mean that we are imbeciles

---

[1] λογίσασθαί excogitare evangelium de nostra mente (**to devise a gospel out of our own mind).**
[2] Cf. Gal. i. 11-12.
[3] Jer. xxxi. 31; Matt. xxvi. 28; Mark xiv. 24; Luke xxii. 20; Heb. chs. vii. viii. ix, x, xii, xiii, especially viii. 10.
[4] γράμμα, Sinai (**at Sinai**): πνεῦμα, Pentecoste (**at Pentecost**).
[5] Cf. Rom. vii. 10. ἡ ἐντολὴ . . . εἰς θάνατον.

in intelligence, that we are to abjure the use of mind. The thought is evidently, as we have shown, that we are wholly incapable of originating a Gospel, or of amending one; of evolving a message out of our own consciousness; of speculating out a Christianity; of telling any man out of our own heads how the ruin of his nature is to be repaired, and the burthen of his guilt to be lifted off, how he is to find strength and power to have victory over the devil, the world, and self, how he is 'to glorify God on earth and to enjoy Him fully for ever'. We cannot *excogitate* answers to these things, as we could in the case, for instance, of many questions of physical or political science. We are by nature dumb and blind before the problems of salvation, before the mystery of guilt and of spiritual impotence. To know what to think about these things, and what to say, is far above our own reach.

But then (the Apostle unfolds this also) we are not below the reach of Him who can enable us to know. He 'hath made us able'. He hath qualified us, capacitated us for His work. Sovereign in skill and power, He has taken us from the dust and ruins of the Fall, and from the thick darkness of our ignorance of Him; has made us what He requires as His instruments, and has taught us what we require for His message. With a *fiat*, as creative as that in Genesis, He 'hath shined in our hearts' (iv. 6), and revealed to us the glory of the sinner's Saviour and the saint's Head. He has quickened us from the death of sin to the life which is hid with Christ in God. He has shown to us, and given to us His Son. He has shown to us, and entrusted to us His Gospel (iv. 7). So, we are able. We know our Master, our message, and our strength.

But of what in particular does the Apostle say that we are 'made able' to be ministers, or 'qualified as agents' as we have paraphrased? Able ministers and qualified agents of the NEW COVENANT. This is our rendering of the word διαθήκη which in every place, or almost every place, of its occurrence in the New Testament, answers better, both by usage and by context, to the idea of a covenant than to the more limited idea of a testamentary will. Here, then, he speaks of himself and his fellows as 'Able ministers of the NEW COVENANT; not of the letter, but of the Spirit; for the letter killeth, but the Spirit giveth life'. Consult the context about the meaning of this 'letter' and this 'Spirit'; and you find that the letter means the holy Law, immovable, graven in the rock for ever, and divinely fatal to the sinner's hopes if he would use it as his title to life; and you find that the Spirit means the Holy Spirit, here named as the crowning and concentrating blessing of the Gospel of our Lord Jesus Christ. 'We preach not,' he means, 'as our distinctive message, the sacred, the divine anathema; we preach Him who has taken it on His own immaculate head, and, in the infinite merit of that sacrifice, now sheds into man's inmost being the Holy Ghost, the Lord, the Life-Giver, to make the new heart, to teach the art and practice of new and saving trust, to sustain in the new life, to prompt the new song, to unfold the New Covenant, to make all things new, from the inmost to the outmost of the man'.

Let us note further the practical lesson of all this for the Christian teacher and pastor. Let him make very much in his instructions, public and private, of the revelation of the Spirit. Let him leave no room, so far as he can do it, for doubt or oblivion in his friends' minds about the absolute necessity of the fullness of the presence and power of the Holy One, if life is to be indeed Christian. Let him describe, as boldly and fully as the Word describes it, what life may be, must be, where that sacred fullness dwells; how assured, how happy within, how serviceable around, how pure, free, and strong, how heavenly, how practical, how humble. Let him at the same time remember that the actual realization of this fullness comes in different ways to different men. But, whilst fully recognizing this, let him also urge any who have yet to learn it, to learn all this in their own experience—claiming on their knees the mighty gift of God.

St. Paul now deals with the contrast between the two Covenants.

What a message of glory therefore; how pure, how great, defame it who will! See its splendour, by contrast ᵠwith the real yet inferior

Ver. 7. splendour of the other message. **For if the agency of the death,** the message which conveyed, practically, only doom to us sinners, that message couched **in written words, stamped[1] upon the stones** of Sinai, **took place** (ἐγενήθη), being uttered and inaugurated, **in** circumstances of **glory;** the face of the human mediator of the Law shone with the splendour he had seen when the Law was given him; **so that the sons of Israel could not bear to look steadily** directing their gaze **upon the** transfigured **face of Moses, by reason of the glory of his** shining **face, though it was destined to decline and**

Ver. 8. **fade** (τὴν καταργουμένην): **how much more then shall not the agency of the Spirit,** the Gospel of The Holy Ghost, be attended **with glory,** albeit not now the glory of visible splendours,

Ver. 9. but of the majesty of holiness? **For if the agency of our condemnation,** killing and spelling death, as we have said, was **glory,** how **much more abundant is the agency of our righteousness,** our free justification,[2] **in** respect of **glory.**[3] Aye, so abundant

Ver. 10. that the glory of the Law, divine as it was, sinks into shadow before it. **For verily the thing glorified stands even stript of glory in this respect,** or, as if it had never been glorified, **because of the yet surpassing glory** of its blessed antithesis. Among other things, the Law was transient, the Gospel is permanent. **So, if that**

Ver. 11. **which was destined to abolition** (i.e. The Law) was attended **with** an equipment and circumstances of **glory, far more** is **that which is** destined **to abide** (i.e. The Gospel)[4] experienced and realized in an atmosphere of glory.

St. Paul has drawn out his contrast between the Covenant of Sinai and the Covenant of the Spirit, especially in respect of the glory which attends upon each. Now he will refer to his ministry and the glory which attends the Gospel ministry, elaborating on the theme of Moses and the veil.

Ver. 12. **Having then such a hope,** a joyful outlook for us of peace, a power here and hereafter through the final message of Divine love, in view of it **we speak with absolute explicitness** in our teaching. Reserve and riddle befitted the symbolic and preparatory

---

[1] Exod. xxxiv. 28. 'He wrote the words of the Covenant'.
[2] Ita Paulus Rom. iii. 25, 26. Justificatio porta est sanctitatis per Spiritum (So **Paul Rom. iii. 25, 26. Justification is the door of holiness through the Spirit).**
[3] Reading ἐν δόξῃ.
[4] Finale est evangelium **(The Gospel is final).**

order of things, but they are out of place when the glorious Finality is
Ver. 13. before us. **And** we, in this our explicit ministry of the New
Covenant, are **not as 'Moses who put a veil on his face'**[1]
—you remember this action of his with the veil, which of itself forms a
parable—**with a view to the sons of Israel not beholding the
end of that which was passing away,** so that they could not see
Ver. 14. clearly that the law was destined in its nature to abolition, and
had an end. They could not see through the veil, **but their
thoughts were dulled,** their spiritual eyes lost sensation, becoming
bleared and nerveless. And the proof is before us, **for to this very day
that same veil,** which is the veiling of the secret that in Christ the Law
is destined to abolition—that veil, **when the Old Covenant is read** in
the Synagogue, **remains** unremoved, **it not being disclosed** to them
Ver. 15. **that it comes to an end in Christ.** So it is indeed; **but even
till now, whenever Moses is read** in their hearing, **a veil
lies over their heart,** over their intellect, affections, and will. **But
Ver. 16 whenever,** as yet it shall do, that heart—the Jewish heart—
shall turn to the Lord, that veil is destined to be **withdrawn.** Then they shall see Him indeed as the end of the Law for
Ver. 17. righteousness to every one that believeth. (And what they
want, for such conversion, is just the Lord, in His full manifestation: **and the Lord,** for such purposes of Grace, **means in effect the**
promised **Spirit** sent by Him to reveal Him. They want liberty—release
from blind misbelief; **and** it is **where that Spirit of the Lord** works
that spiritual **liberty** is, and nowhere else). Such is Israel's state and
Ver. 18. need. **But** with us believers, how different is the case, for **we
all** stand as it were where Moses stood, but before a brighter
glory, the Gospel-splendour; **from our face the veil is lifted off, we
reflect as a mirror the glory of the Lord Christ**[2] on our brow, **we
are transforming** in that blessed sunshine **into the same image,
from glory to glory,**[3] from stage to stage of likeness to Himself, in
way and measure **true to** the working of none less than **the Lord the
Spirit;** that is practically Christ, indeed made Christ to us by the Holy
Ghost.[4]

So the Apostle ends these thoughts with reference to the
glory which comes from God Himself and returns to Him from
every true ministry of the New Covenant. Let us go forth in the

---

[1] Exodus xxxiv. 33.
[2] The sense 'We see, as reflected in a mirror, the Lord's glory' is possible
—the mirror of the Word.
[3] Mirum! **(A wonder?).**
[4] Jesus Christ res est Pentecostes **(Jesus Christ is the substance of
Pentecost).**

name of the Son of God to this our ministry. Let us advance to
our whole work with all our aims and thoughts simplified into
this; that we are set, by grace, upon glorifying God in this ministry
of the Covenant.

Let this be the last word upon our souls, that deep, holy, immortal aim, to glorify God. 'Supernatural is the desire to glorify
God', wrote that great saint, Henry Venn the elder: 'it is the
bud and blossom which brings forth all the fruit the Church of
God bears'. The Lord lead us forth in peace thus to do His will,
in His rest, and in His strength, till we lie down to die into His
presence. Then may we take our Master's words, in our humble
measure, upon our failing lips: 'I have glorified Thee upon the
earth: I have finished the work which Thou gavest me to do'.

Chapter v

THE POWER UPON CHRISTIAN WORKERS OF A PRESENT INDWELLING OF CHRIST

2 Corinthians iv. 1-15

ST. PAUL is writing an Epistle which pre-eminently discloses to us himself, the very man, the human heart beating at the centre of that immense circumference of enterprise, and only quickened into warmer and more manifold sensibility by the indwelling of the Holy Ghost. To the Corinthians, whom he loved, and who loved him well, yet perplexed and grieved him too, he presents his whole self, without even the thinnest artificial veil. Affection, hope, disappointment, indignation, irony, bitter rebuke, tenderest entreaty—all comes out precisely as it is felt, in the utterance of a devotion to them which has nothing to conceal.

In the course of such a message so delivered he comes to the paragraph before us. And here he dilates awhile upon the great phenomenon of the Christian Ministry, its message, its motives, the divine energies which can alone sustain the minister, the illumination which his own spirit must needs receive if he is to shed the light of Christ around him.

Such is the Gospel. Denied, opposed, maligned, it has but to be re-stated in its sacred radiance to be defended and to prevail. And **because**
Ver. 1. **of this, holding** as we do **this agency** (διακονίαν), in the further-ance of the cause of such a Gospel, **even as mercy alone made us so,**[1] turning us from its foes to its devotees, so too with that mercy still warm in our hearts, **we do not lose courage** (ἐγκακεῖν),
Ver. 2. hard as is the struggle with opposing foes. **But,** as we have said, we have parted from the first with all reserves, prevarica-

---

[1] ἠλεήθημεν—aorist.

26

tions, or side-long aims, for our message is nothing if not light as day, and when **we** took it up we of course **definitely renounced the secrets of shame** (i.e. things to be hushed up because we should be shamed by their disclosure) **as those who cannot** (μὴ) **walk** and live and act **in craft,** and without principle, **nor adulterate¹ the message of our** (τοῦ) God. **But by the spreading wide open** (τῇ φανερώσει) **of the** glorious **Truth** we seek **to substantiate our claim** as authentic messengers **before every human conscience, in the presence of** the all-seeing God. Is it objected that for all this our distinctive Gospel remains a

Ver. 3.   riddle to many hearts even at Corinth, and that so, after all, it may be a mistake? We must solemnly reply that **if our Gospel** message **is** still **wearing a veil** then **it is wearing a veil** only in² the souls of **those who are on the way to perish;³ in whom** the dark

Ver. 4.   Power who is **the God of this age,⁴** spirit-ruler⁵ of those who live for time and not for heaven, **did blind,** when they yielded to his temptations to doubt, **the thoughts⁶ of such unbelieving ones, so that there should not dawn** upon them **the illumination** shed **by the good tidings of the glory of our** (τοῦ) **Christ, who is our** (τοῦ) **God's**

Ver. 5.   **image.**⁷ For just *that* actually is our message, the glory of Christ. **It is not ourselves we are heralding,** as some assert we do, **but Christ, Jesus, as Lord;** the true Messiah, the ever blessed Man, the divine Master; **as for ourselves,** we herald ourselves **as just your slaves, on account of,** for the sake of, **Jesus,** who has

Ver. 6.   given us to live for you. His glory, and that only we must preach. **Because it is** no less than **God Himself, He who said of old, 'Out of darkness light shall shine',⁸ who shone in our hearts,⁹** shone with the ray of the manifested beauty of His dear Son, **with a view to** our shedding forth from that dark region¹⁰ **the illumination** which communicates and consists **of the knowledge of the glory of God** seen **in the face of** Jesus Christ;¹¹ His moral glory, the pure splendour of truth and love, made visible in the Saviour, incarnate and sacrificed, in His personal and living grace.¹²

---

¹ So λίβανον (Matt. ii. 11 and Rev. xviii. 13 only). He does not adulterate the frankincense of devotion into the frankincense of merchandise.

² Cf. ἐν ταῖς καρδίαις ἡμῶν ver. 6.   ³ Cf. ii. 15.

⁴ Cf. the tone of 1 John iv. 5, 6. 'They are of the world', etc.

⁵ Cf. Eph. ii. 2.   ⁶ Contrast Phil. iv. 7.

⁷ Cf. Col. i. 15; Heb. i. 3.

⁸ λάμψει Gen. i. 2, 3, freely rendered.

⁹ Cf. Gal. i. 16.

¹⁰ ita ut nos lucem demus aliis (**So that we may give light to others**).

¹¹ aurora caelestis (**heavenly dawn**).

¹² For this vs. cf. Num. xiv. 21 of The Father of Glory: Isaiah xi. 2-9 of The Spirit of Knowledge: Hab. ii. 14 (=2 Cor. iv. 6) of The Son of God. (Ed.)

'Ourselves as just your slaves for the sake of Jesus'. Such is this great Christian worker's central and ultimate conception of the Christian Ministry. He has much to say about it, elsewhere, from other sides; about its commission and authority, and about the moral dignity of its idea. But here he lays his hand upon its very heart, and gives us the central glory of the thing. And the words denote the most absolute antithesis possible to every thought of an ecclesiastical assumption, to all such self-exaltation of a ministerial class or order as can harden it into that far different thing, for which the Christianity of the apostles has no place, a hierarchical caste. The words delightfully negative all that is connoted by that term of mournful omen, as of mournful history, *clericalism*. They present to us in short a conception not magisterial but altogether ministerial. The pastor, teacher, and guide in things divine has here no ambition outside the glory of his heavenly Master. And within that sacred limit his supreme ambition is to be, in Christ, the bondservant of his brethren. He belongs to them, not they to him. He recognizes ever, and with joy, that the Church is greater than the Ministry. The Bride of the Lamb is greater than the bondman of the Bride.

So the man's whole life is at once chastened and dignified by his call to a high ambition, which by the law of its nature is altogether pure. To 'proclaim Christ Jesus as Lord', that is the hope which animates him every day. He lives to make Christ great to human hearts. He lives 'that Christ may be magnified in his body', that Christ may look out at the windows of his life and may beckon from its doors. Only, as we shall see, the figure which he uses is not that of the open casement but rather of broken earthenware, the better befitting the shattering experience from which he has recently emerged.

Thus it is a surpassingly glorious message. But do you object that its messengers are poor creatures? That I, for example, am frail and often miserably ill? Well, be it so; weak, battered, wearing-out mortal; perfectly true. But this is only a foil to the message. **We have**
Ver. 7.   as a fact **this treasure,** a glorious Christ for men, **in vessels of earthenware,** like Gideon's pitchers,[1] broken to show the lamps

---

[1] Judges vii.

within, and this with a purpose—**that the grandeur,** the pre-eminence **of the power,**[1] manifested in spiritual triumphs, **may be** seen to be **our God's, and not originated in us.** Truly the earthenware is battered

Ver. 8.   and broken; yet always with a glorious counterpart, showing God in us; we are **on every side afflicted, but not driven to the wall; at a loss but not at a hopeless loss; persecuted,** chased

Ver. 9.   by opposition, **but not left in the lurch** by our divine leader; **thrown** ever and again (present) **to the ground, but not perishing** even there; **always carrying about, in our body,** as we

Ver. 10.   sustain these assaults on limbs and on feelings, **the death-process of our Jesus;** an experience akin to that in which He gave Himself up to the deadly blows of circumstance culminating in the cross; and this, not just for the sake of suffering, but **that in this same body of ours,** through these physical frames and these sensibilities, thus belaboured yet thus upborne, **the life too of our Jesus may be** manifested, or rather **displayed;**[2] the world seeing proof that our Master is risen, and lives indeed, as His power and presence shine out of the earthen vessel's chinks.   For such indeed is the concurrence in our

Ver. 11.   experience of these deep opposites, life and death; **for always we, the living ones** that we are, alive indeed with the indwelling Christ, **are being given over to death,** placed in circumstances which seem like one long martyrdom, and often like its actual close, **on account of Jesus,** for His sake and in His work, but still with this aim in the will of God, **that the life too of that Jesus may be displayed in our mortal flesh;** may be seen plainly to be a fact, for nothing less can explain such joy and power in men whose physical exposure to suffering would otherwise mean nothing less than death itself.

The Second Epistle to the Corinthians is no fitful rhapsody of troubled feeling. All bears upon the rescue of the disciples back from misbeliefs to the eternal truth, from confusion to a strong cohesion in the Lord, from themselves to Christ, to holiness, to heaven. Into the line of that great purpose the apostle has poured not his reasonings only, not even his entreaties, but himself. He has spent upon his converts his own innermost being. He has given to them his soul. Now he will speak in conclusion of the power which makes all these things possible in him, and also

---

[1] Cf. xii. 9.
[2] Ver. 10. Cf. Phil. i. 20.

in them—the power upon Christian workers of a present indwelling of Christ.

Ver. 12. **So then,** to sum up the matter, here are life and death at work; and, from one great view-point, **the death is operating in us;** we are called to the mortal suffering; **but the life is operating in you.** You, thanks to the God who has visited you, in us, have caught the life, have found the Indwelling Christ who now grows in you; you are grandly alive, and without our special call to suffer. And we, meanwhile, go on, full of cheer, with our witness and our labour; with faith Ver. 13. for our secret—faith, that is to say, a trusted Christ. **Having the Spirit of faith,** the Holy Ghost, inspiring us with saving reliance, **the same**[1] Spirit which worked in the Psalmist **according to the word written** in Psalm cxvi. 10, **'I believed, therefore I speak';** my utterance of praise and witness is but the voice of my faith in my God; **we too are believing,** relying, and on an eternal strength; **therefore also we are speaking** this Gospel, which is just the trusted Christ and His blessings as such. **We know**[2] that our struggle Ver. 14. cannot last for ever; death somehow must be its close; but faith bids us also know that there shall be a glorious resurrection; yes we know **that He who raised the Lord Jesus** from His apparent utter death **will raise us too,**[3] us who are joined to Him and follow Him, will raise us **with Jesus and will present us** in His own glorious Ver. 15. presence, as His risen ones—aye, and not alone, it will be **with you,** dear converts and children. **For these things, all of them,** all the troubles, all the mercies, of our lot, **are on your account,** in your interests, for the promotion of your souls' good, your growth in grace; **that the grace, risen to a height,** as it runs **through the more,**[4] through the majority of you whom we see it fills, **may cause the resulting thanksgiving to run over, to the glory of our** (τοῦ) **God.**

In conclusion let us heed the earnest plea, in the interests of true Christian service, for what we need so specially in these hurrying times: a deeper entrance of our souls into the secret of the presence of the Lord, which is the secret of His power upon us.

A servant of Christ in the past, Lucius von Machtholf, was a

---

[1] Sc. eadem atque antiqua illa fides (**that same ancient faith**).

[2] per fidem (**through faith**).

[3] He expects death, cf. John vi. 40, 44, etc.

[4] 1 Cor. ix. 19 and perhaps 2 Cor. ix. 2.

man singularly rich in the gift of spiritual influence over individuals. When asked to disclose something of his secret he
replied, 'I know no other tactics than first of all to be heartily
satisfied with my God, even if He should favour me with no
sensible visible blessing in my vocation. It were better to be sick
in a tent under a burning sun, and Jesus sitting at the tent door,
than to be enchanting a thousand listeners where Jesus was not.
Never let your inner life get low in your search for the lives of
others'. His reply, in essence, was that the secret lay, as far as
he knew, in the sense of profound contentment with His blessed
Master in which his soul was kept through grace. Jesus Christ
irradiated him within and for himself. He was, at the very centre
of his soul's consciousness, deeply happy to belong to his King
who had saved him, and to be used by that great and holy Possessor as should seem best to Him. And this took friction and
anxiety out of his life in a very wonderful way, while it kept that
life, so to speak, always directed, peacefully and unwearily, towards
the thought of service, towards the idea of being used. And the
service was all the happier, because it was not the source of the
man's happiness. The source and secret was Jesus Christ; and
that secret acted equally whether marked success attended speech
and action, or apparently no success at all; whether the servant
was put by the Master into the front rank of active reapers in the
harvest field, or told to sit down in a corner and sharpen the
sickles of others; whether he was called to speak in spiritual
power to a multitude, or to lie still on a sick bed.

We must live upon Jesus Christ. We must, in the rule and
habit of our lives, watch over times of solemn, sacred, blessed
intercourse with Him in secret. We must, despite all the influences of our day, make time for thoughtful prayer, for reverent
search into His Word, for recollection of our treasures in Him,
time to exercise the more deliberate acts of a living faith in His
great promises, and in the unseen realities of the things eternal.

In a Litany of the Moravian Church the petition occurs:
'From the loss of our glory in Thee; from self-complacency; preserve

us, gracious Lord and God'. Such prayers are sorely needed by
the Christian worker and minister today. It is fatally easy to
think that we are living up to our creed when our creed is held
without life—a thing far different from the creed of the glory and
salvation of Christ so known by the soul that it holds the holder.

When we see HIM in deed and in truth, what words can fully
tell the gladness and the freedom? But in that same consciousness,
as we behold Him, we are made aware in our inmost soul of our
own unworthiness, and of the progress to which we are always
called, in a perpetual repentance.

'From all loss of our glory in Thee, preserve and keep us—us
who humbly ask to serve Thee for ever—gracious Lord and
God'.

Chapter vi

THE PROSPECT, EVEN IMMEDIATELY ON DEATH, OF THE ENJOYMENT OF HIS IMMEDIATE PRESENCE[1]

2 Corinthians iv. 16-v. 8

ST. PAUL, as he writes, is describing to his Corinthian converts his own ministerial life, just as it is passing at the time. He comes now to one great personal aspect of it. His 'outward man', his physical frame and system, in the wear and tear of the Lord's work, was 'perishing', decaying; from the bodily point of view he was ageing, he was gradually giving way. But from the other side, from the inner side, the opposite was going on. His 'inward man', his unseen world of will, affection, thought, under the living power of the Spirit of God, making Christ present in his heart by faith, was 'being renewed', being made quite fresh and new. It was not only kept going, somehow maintained in some sort of tolerable working order, beating on like an old clock not quite worn out. It was 'being made new'; filled ever afresh with a strong, bright, life, quickened with a wonderful youth, from a source, a spring, 'full of immortality'. And this was taking place 'day by day'. It was not a matter of one great crisis, or of a few such times. He was not lifted intermittently into new life, and then allowed to sink slowly back to spiritual exhaustion, to be animated once again. It was a matter of 'day by day'. He lived a day at a time in regard to the work, the suffering, the battle, and a day at a time in regard to the 'being made new'.

Ver. 16. So, as we said above (ver. 1), **we do not lose courage,** hard as the warfare of the Gospel is; **no, even though** (εἰ καὶ) **our external man,** our being in that part, that surface, which circumstance can wear, tire, and wound, **is wearing out, still our internal man**

---

[1] For further reading on this significant subject see *Thoughts for the Sundays of the Year*, ch. xxxvi and xxxvii; *Christ's Witness to the Life to Come*, ch. xi; *Christus Consolator*, ch. ix to end.

(ὁ ἔσω ἡμῶν),[1] our being in the region where faith, hope, and love move
Ver. 17. and work, **is being renovated** by the Lord's indwelling life
day by day, a day at a time. **For** that renovation evidences
itself, works itself out, in precisely this—the exercise of the faith which is
the substance of things hoped for, the demonstration of things not seen,
and so of a hope which makes not ashamed; so that, viewed thus, we
realize with ever new cheer that **the momentary light**[2] load **of our
tribulation, in overwhelming measures,** 'on the scale of excess upon
excess', **is working out**[3] **for us,** developing for us, **an eternal weight
of glory,** heavy with the treasures of heaven, and interminable as heaven
itself; in which every sorrow borne for Christ will be found to have
made us capable of some special gift of bliss and power; the condition
to such an issue being, on our side, a right attitude and regard, **we not
Ver. 18. having regard to the things in sight, but to the things
out of sight;** and this rightly indeed, **for the things in sight
are temporary,**[4] **but the things out of sight are eternal,** boundless
in duration. And this we say with special reference to the unseen bliss
hereafter of the faithful servant here.

The Apostle in these verses is engaged in matters of personal
experience. He is explaining to his converts, as a true pastor
will sometimes care to do, certain secrets of his activity in itself
so exhausting, so wearing, nay, if we may use the word, so lacer-
ating in its course of toils and sufferings, but which finds him
nevertheless always ready to go on. The Apostle's life might be
illustrated by that remarkable scene in the *Pilgrim's Progress*
where the Interpreter, in his house of parables, takes the Traveller
in to watch the fire which burns on ever brighter under difficulties.
There is the glowing hearth, always more alive with flame. Yet
in front of it stands one who continually casts water on the heat,
to put it out. Christian is much perplexed. Then his host leads
him round behind the wall, and lo! another agent is at work there,
pouring through a secret channel oil into the fire. So the paradox
is explained.

Thus it was with St. Paul's life, and the forces which threatened
hard to bear it down. Behind it, within it, was 'the secret of the

---

[1] Rom. vii. 22, Eph. iii. 16. Contrast Rom. vi. 6 (παλαιός) and Col. iii. 9, 10
(παλαιός and νέος).
[2] Ita nunc reverâ Beatis videtur (**So now in fact it appears to the Blessed**).
[3] Cf. Phil. ii. 13, et infra v. 5.
[4] Matt. xiii. 21; Heb. xi. 25; cf. Philem. 15.

Lord'. The veil of tired and suffering humanity held concealed below it, beating with immortality, the life of Jesus. And while the man felt and handled 'the things seen', and sometimes endured and sometimes wonderfully used them, he saw, with the open eyes of the soul, not them but the things unseen, the things eternal, as the true landscape of his life. 'For this cause' he did 'not faint'. 'The outward man', he admits, was 'perishing'. But it did not matter. 'The inward man', the pulse of the machine 'was renewing day by day'. Let us realize afresh, that there is such a 'secret of the Lord', and that it is for us today, if indeed we are His disciples. It is a talisman as potent in the twentieth century as in the first. Now as then the eternal Master claims our whole devotion, in whatever path it is to be shown. Now as then, world, flesh, and devil cross that path at every turn, and make the Christian life not only difficult but impossible, if we try to live it of ourselves. But now as then the oil of heaven is ready to run in from behind the wall. 'The life of Jesus', the living Lord dwelling in the heart, can still prove inexhaustible, victorious, 'in the mortal flesh'. The things which are not seen can be still brought within the spirit's sight, and then that which is impossible with man is, in man, found possible with God.

This is no poor plausible theory, fit for a reverie, annihilated by real life. Who has not known examples of it, modern as ourselves? There was the mother, given wholly to every duty of domestic love, yet also wholly instinct with the unearthly power of her beloved Saviour's presence. There was the friend, alive to every problem of his period, practical and laborious in its service, yet for whom the mastering and empowering passion, elastic with eternal life, was always Jesus Christ. There was that other friend, put to fiery proof in the extremes of pain and weakness, yet still lifted by an unseen embrace above them, calm to the end, and cheerful, and full of thought for others, and all because the Lord was with him and was in him; so he would affirm with indescribable simplicity and joy.

The facts of conquering faith are no antiquarian study. The living specimens of the immortal race are around us. The life of Jesus and the things unseen are modern as well as ancient,

contemporary always, because they are eternal; 'the same yester-
day, and today, and for ever'. And for us, for every one of us,
it is intended that those forces should be our own. The old
baptismal prayer is a nobly true petition for every real member
of Christ without exception; not that we may 'walk in a vain
shadow' of the Christian life, that but we may have 'power and
strength to have victory, and may triumph against the devil,
the world, and the flesh'.

But it is time to return to our paraphrase.

Ver. 1.   **For we know,** with the certainty of faith reposing upon revelation, **that, even if our terrestrial house of the tent,** our
mortal body, the spirit's residence on earth, and tentlike in its frailty
and removableness, **shall be taken down** ('struck' in death), **we have
a structure,**[1] strong and permanent, **derived from God** as its immediate
giver, **a house not made with hands,**[2] not of material framework, and
so not subject to the law 'composita solventur' (the elements are dis-
solved), **eternal** in duration, and **in the heavens** for its region of origin.

Ver. 2.   Such a prospect is all important to us; we cannot rest in things
as they are; **for in this,** this tent of the mortal body, **we are
groaning,**[3] with the double consciousness of its actual frailty, and
liability to ruin, and exposure to inward evils, and of the contrast of all
this to what is waiting for us, **yearning**[4] with home-sick hearts **to put on**
the over-robe[5] of **our habitation which belongs to heaven** (ἐξ οὐρανοῦ)
and will come from it for each redeemed one at the Lord's return; the
heavenly envelope of our being, which will in one respect—that of con-
cealing—be to the mortal body as the ἐπενδύτης to the under-garment,

Ver. 3.   though unlike it in this that it will not merely conceal it, but
take its place; **if** (εἰ γε)[6] **at the act of** (καὶ) **putting it on we shall
not be found,**[7] surprised by the sudden and wonderful crisis, **naked,** un-
clothed of the mortal σκῆνος and disembodied; for these longings do not
annul the law of our nature, by which man, created first in the body and
then in the soul, abhors the thought of disembodiment. So we, by in-

---

[1] 'structura' illa nihil ponderis habet (**that 'frame' has no heaviness**).
[2] ἀχειροποίητος Mark xiv. 58; Col. ii. 11; only in the N.T.
[3] Rom. viii. 23.
[4] Cf. Rom. xv. 23; 2 Cor. ix. 14; Phil. ii. 24, 26; iv. 1.
[5] Cf. ἐπενδύτης John xxi. 7.
[6] εἰ γε=if. Cf. εἴπερ=if only.
[7] Cf. Phil. iii. 9; aliter Phil. ii. 8.

stinctive preference, would rather be clothed over the present body with
the future, than step out of the present body and have to pass to
the future body across however brief a void.[1] **For,** returning to
our previous avowal, **we,** dwellers **as we are in the tent, are
groaning, as under a burthen,** the burthen of the encumbrance and
limitations, aye, and the defilements of mortality;[2] **only with this proviso,**[3]
that we do not want and indeed **are unwilling** (οὐ θέλομεν) **to take** this
clothing off, but rather desire **to put** other **clothing on,** as will be the case at
The Lord's Return to His yet living servants, **that so the mortal may
be absorbed by** and so disappear into the **life;** the mortal body vanish-
ing, not into thin air, but into the already received glory of the
immortal body. **Well, He who worked us out** (almost
worked us up), took us as bad material in our fallen state, and by His
transforming grace wrought us into new creatures **for that very** goal or
end, namely the fullness of the final glory whether attained by the darker
or the brighter passage, **is God** and none less than He. The Worker is
indeed adequate to the work, and besides we have a pledge from Him
that His idea shall be realized—**He Who did give us,** when He gave us
salvation, **the earnest,** the gift in hand, the payment on account, **of The
Spirit,** which is indeed the personal endowment of The Holy Ghost
Himself as the secret of joy, purity, and power in a new life whose
natural outcome is glory (cf. Rom. viii. 11).

Ver. 4.

Ver. 5.

Wonderful is this deep characteristic of the Scripture; its
Gospel, for the body, with which St. Paul is here dealing. In
Christ, the body is seen to be something far different from the
mere clog, or prison, or chrysalis, of the soul. It is its destined
implement, may we not say its mighty wings in prospect, for the
life of glory. As invaded by sin, it must needs pass through
either death or, at the Lord's Return, an equivalent transfiguration. But as created in God's plan of Human Nature it is for
ever congenial to the soul, nay, it is necessary to the soul's full
action. And whatever be the mysterious mode (it is absolutely
hidden from us as yet) of the event of the Resurrection, this we

---

[1] The whole passage is of course highly figurative in its terms, and in its
essence quite consonant with the different terms of Phil. iii. 20, 21 and 1 Cor.
xv. 51f.—where meanwhile v. 53 closely approximates to this passage in terms,
only it uses the more abstract words ἀφθαρσίαν, ἀθανασίαν. On the question,
'Does this all mean an articulate expectation that he, Paul, would see the
Advent?' I would rather be silent. I do not think, however, that it does. (Cf.
John xxi ult.)

[2] 'ce fardeau de chagrins' (**this load of sorrows**).

[3] ἐφ' ᾧ (ἐφ' ᾧτε=on condition that).

know, that the glory of the immortal body will have profound
relations with the work of God in the sanctified soul. It will be
because of the earnest of the Spirit already given and 'because
of the Spirit dwelling in you', as your power for holiness in
Christ.

So the Christian reads the account of his present spiritual
wealth, and of his coming completed life, 'his perfect consummation and bliss in the eternal glory'. Let him reverence his
mortal body, even while he 'keeps it in subjection', and while he
willingly tires it, or gives it to suffer, for his Lord. For it is the
temple of the Spirit. It is the casket of the hope of glory.

St. Paul now describes the faithful Christian's hope.

What a prospect is thus before us, and what a warrant of its reality
we possess! Aye, we need not too anxiously desire the alternative of
being alive at His Coming, and so escaping death. Our New Creator,

Ver. 6. our divine Earnest, will take care that in either event all shall
be well. So (οὖν), **with hearts of cheer always,** come joy or
sorrow, come life, come death—**and knowing** as we do **that, while we
are at home in the body,** however we may fear to quit it, **we are** away
from home from the Lord, not yet 'with Christ' (Phil. i. 23) in that
immediate presence which is 'far better' than the best here; I mean

Ver. 7. **because** here, as a fact, **we are walking,** living and acting
by means of faith, by reliance on an unseen Promiser, **and
not[1] by means of Object Visible,[2]** as we shall do beyond the veil

Ver. 8. where in the heavenly rest we shall with inconceivable direct-
ness *see* the Lord Jesus—**to resume** (δὲ) I say, **we have hearts
of cheer, and** now, choosing as far as in us lies, **deliberately approve,
rather,[3]** as against the best of the present lot, **to quit** (aorist) **the body**
as our home at death, cost what it may, **and to get home with the
Lord** (literally 'to get home towards the Lord' and so to go *to* Him to be
with Him, cf. 2 Thess. iii. 1, 'Chez vous': also John i. 1).

---

[1] οὐ—'Ergo ibi videmus corpore dissoluto' (**therefore we see there, even
though the body is disintegrated**).

[2] Species (**that which is seen**) (Vulg.) σωματικὸν εἶδος Luke iii. 22.

[3] Cf. ἐπιθυμία Phil. i. 23. Vide Philippian Studies. *in loc.*

In these few verses we have some of the most precious dis-
closures in all Scripture of the sequel of the Christian's death.
Let us set out reverently a few of these guarded and sparing
truths. They concern the beauties of that wonderful morn when
the pilgrim finally strikes his tent and moves into his eternal home.

1. At death the spirit leaves the mortal body. The conscious
self is 'absent from the body' or 'leaves its home in the body'.
Between death and resurrection *that* connexion is broken. But
we are not to assume for certain that the outgoer is therefore
formless, bodiless. It may be that the passage we have
covered teaches that an 'envelope' will be provided at once for
the faithful soul, and we incline to think that it does. In that
case the body of the resurrection will be, so to speak, the efflor-
escence of that envelope and continuous with it and with the present
body, by the identity of the wearer, the subject. We dare not
pronounce with certainty. But the angels have power to 'materi-
alize' a bodily vehicle. So the human spirit, yonder, may well
have a similar privilege, the possession of an organ for its life and
action, pending the resurrection glory.

2. That beyond the veil *light* reigns we are to be quite sure.
Whittier is true to revelation when he says that

> 'Death is a covered way which opens into light.'

It is a tunnel, a very short tunnel, with a summer landscape at
the far end. On the outside of the tunnel the whole day is shining
all the while. And the day is breaking already, from the end, into
the darkness underneath the roof.[1]

Wonderful visions have been given of that light, now and then
to passing souls. A Scottish believer, strong, self-restrained, a
characteristic son of the Presbyterian Church, Dr. Kalley,

---

[1] 'My friend Mr. Thomason in his dying hour said, "There is a long, dark
vista, but there is light at the end". His Mother being reminded of that in her
last hour, replied, "No, it is light to me all the way".'—Carus' *Memoirs of
Simeon*, 3rd edition, p. 550.(Ed.).

approached his end, an aged man. As a veteran medical practitioner, he calmly told his wife, how he must expect to die suddenly, but that he hoped to give her notice. One day he laid his hand on her arm, said the words, 'Oh, my dear wife!' and immediately expired. The words and his manner, said Mrs. Kalley, were precisely those with which, years before, during a tour they took in the Highlands, he touched her arm and bade her look, when suddenly a mountain view of entrancing grandeur broke upon them.

3. There will be light there, and so indeed there will be *sight*. This is revealed in many places in the Book, and so also in the pregnant passage we have now covered where St. Paul discourses of the 'dissolution' of 'the earthly house of this tabernacle', and the sequel. Quite incidentally he says of our present state, *as contrasted with the state after dissolution*, that 'we walk by faith, not by sight', or as we have paraphrased with more precision, 'not by Object Visible'. The holy logic works out to the conclusion that there, 'absent from the body', the Christian does 'walk by Object Visible'. He sees, he sees indeed.

4. But the supreme and crowning certainty about the Christian's life after death is summed up in two words—'WITH CHRIST'. That was the Lord's own promise from the Cross. It was made, let us remember, not to a Stephen, not to a John, but to the dying thief: 'Today shalt thou be in Paradise', in the heavenly Garden, 'with me'. Wonderful is that word 'Paradise', charged with every radiant idea of the beautiful in the environment of the soul. But the living sun, which makes the glory of it all, is these words, 'with me'. So it is again and again, in many passages which we might likewise take for meditation.   'To depart, and to be with Christ' (Phil. i. 23). 'We are willing to leave home in the body and to get home to the Lord'. The ultimate bliss of resurrection has no higher promise in kind than this promise of the intermediate state: 'So shall we ever be with the Lord'. (1 Thess. iv. 17).

What must the results be of that holy and unclouded company-keeping! What depths and heights of growth! What outshining more and more of the likeness of the Beloved in the lover, of the Worshipped in the happy worshipper!

> Aye, think of all things at the best; in one fair thought unite
> All purest joys of sense and soul, all earthly love and light;
> Bid Hope and Memory meet at length and knit their wreaths in one;
> And o'er them shed the tenderest light of Fancy's inner Sun;
>
> Yet bind the truth upon thy brow and clasp it to thy heart,
> And then nor grief nor gladness here shall claim too great a part—
> All radiance of this lower sky is to that glory dim;
> Far better to depart it is, for we shall be with Him.

Chapter vii

THE PROSPECT OF THE GREAT 'JUDICIUM DOMESTICUM' WHICH HE WILL HOLD—HIS TRIBUNAL FOR HIS SERVANTS

2 Corinthians v. 9-10

WE have considered the blissful day of the Christian's entry into the Heavenly Home to be 'with Christ' for ever. The two verses we now paraphrase have to do with some of the more serious questions and answers *within the house* of Christ in the Unseen. This is not so much a universal judgement-hour, which is assuredly to come with its dread appeal to a universal conscience. Rather is it an investigation within the family circle of the disciples; a *forum domesticum*; the Lord's particular scrutiny of His servant-brethren; His enquiry into them, as such, how they have lived for Him; how they have used life for Him, in its powers and occasions; how for Him they have acted and behaved themselves not merely in but through the body; what for Him they have gained by trading with the resources He has committed to them, the golden talents of time, of health, of wealth, of thought, of will, of affection, of society, of the means and opportunities all and sundry for His service through the body.

In view of all this which he includes in his prospect of the Heavenly Home, St. Paul states his own ambition, the mark of his noblest aspirations.

Such then, again, is the wealth of our blessings, present and to come. The contemplation of them does but quicken our desire to be true to the Giver. **Wherefore also we have a** holy **ambition,**[1] Ver. 9. **whether we be at home or from home,** as regards the

---

[1] φιλοτιμούμεθα—Sancta ambitio (**Holy ambition**).

body, as regards the Lord, when He comes again to pronounce upon His servants' work, **to meet His approval.**

The Apostle here expresses a deep purpose of his life; it is that, 'whether present or absent', that is to say, whether out of the body or in it when the Lord calls him to examination, he may be 'accepted of Him', or more literally 'to meet His approval'. This is his 'ambition'. For this is one of the passages where the Greek equivalent to ambition occurs; 'wherefore we are ambitious', is the precisely literal translation.

Now he goes on to expand that prospect and its conditions in the next verse. He anticipates a definite occasion on which may be expressed the 'approval' of which he is 'ambitious'. There is coming a time when his Lord will summon him, as He will summon all who serve Him, to a 'judgement-seat', where a scrutiny will be conducted into what has been 'done through the body', and at which the Lord will express His opinion of the doing, and will award accordingly.

Ver. 10. **For** we have this also in prospect, the Master's scrutiny of His household; His *forum domesticum*, where He enquires what they have gained by trading:[1] **we must, all of us, be displayed**[2] just as we have been, and just as we have done, every veil removed, **in front of the tribunal of our** (τοῦ) **Christ,** that He may inspect and may pronounce, **so that each may get** the result of **the things done by means of the body,**[3] the service rendered by means of limb and faculty in the earthly life, **with regard to just what he did** as a servant, **whether good or worthless.**[4] There, perhaps, we and those who now oppose us, must alike stand.

When we view these verses as a whole we find a striking parallel in the earlier epistle in 1 Cor. iii. 11-15. There we have the

---

[1] Matt. xxv. 21.
[2] Cf. 1 Cor. iii. 13.
[3] διὰ τοῦ σώματος—usum corporalium facultatum pro Domino (**the use of bodily faculties for the Lord**).
[4] On φαῦλος see Trench, *New Testament Synonyms* § lxxxiv.

thought of a fiery test to be applied hereafter, not to the persons but to the works of labourers for God. All are supposed to have 'built upon the foundation'. All are supposed to be 'saved'. But how they have worked, what they have done as builders for the King, is, nevertheless, put to test. Have they piled up a structure of precious metal and stones, or have they reared what is only fit to be food for the fire? 'Of what sort' has been their work? Accordingly as 'the fire' answers that query, so does the worker, as a worker, 'receive' or not receive a 'reward'; he hears or he does not hear, 'Well done, good and faithful'.

When we look more closely in detail at the paraphrase one or two of the renderings will help us better to realize the significance of these verses. 'We must all appear' (A.V.) may better be rendered 'we must all be displayed', or 'manifested'. The thought is not merely that of attending at a summons, of putting in an appearance, an *adsum*, a formal muster before the Prince's chair. It is that of being disclosed, examined, under a broad light, so as to seem just what we are. It is to be a showing up of all that the Christian has come to be through the use of faculty and circumstance, a disclosure and display of it before his Master, and his fellow-servants, and himself. Again 'the things done in the body' (A.V.) should rather read 'the things done by means of the body' or 'through the body'; this is the only literal rendering of the Greek. The thought is that of the body as the implement of action, the vehicle of faculties and energies, the talent, so to speak, which has been laid out and used.

And how can conduct, in its development, be more vividly presented to our thought, or more significantly than as the things done through the body? For, speaking practically and as to the breadth of experience, our conduct in human life on earth— what we are, as this is developed through what we do and how we behave—is a thing which asserts itself naturally through the body. It is altogether through the body, in the vast range of common experience, that we act and are acted upon in our present state. Our duties are done, our influences are exerted, the influences from around us are received in their moulding power, our purposes are carried out, with all the reflected effect on us of the accomplishment, or of the attempt—through the body. It is through the body that we are members of human society. It is through the body that in that society we use, or misuse, every capacity, every gift, every trust, material or immaterial, lodged for a season in our keeping.

Nothing is more significantly characteristic of the Gospel than its profound regard for the body. According to it, the body of the Christian man is already 'the temple of the Holy Ghost'; and it is hereafter to be transfigured into a condition kindred to that of the body of his risen Lord. And meantime he is besought, he is commanded, to 'glorify God in his body': to make it his daily ambition 'that Christ may be magnified in his body': to 'present his body a living sacrifice, holy, acceptable; his reasonable service'; that is to say, the vehicle of his worshipping reason's life for God.

All this in regard to the body is here taken by St. Paul in full view of the investigation within the family circle to which we have already referred. What does it not say, thus taken, to the conscience of the man who has in any sense confessed that Christ is Lord, and has any apprehension, if but the most confused, of his Lord's rights upon him, and has begun in any measure to know himself? What can he say in the prospect? 'Enter not into judgement with Thy servant, O Lord'. Well, for sublime reasons of His own, because of His own bearing of His servants' sins on His own head, He will not enter into hostile judgement with him. In *that* respect, by an amnesty of immeasurable mercy, those 'sins and iniquities He will remember no more'. But He will assuredly enter into scrutiny with His servant, as to the use he has made of himself for his Redeemer. He will most certainly ask him what he has done through his body, aright or amiss, as responsible to Jesus Christ.

Intimations of the awe of that enquiry seem to come to us not from the words of Revelation only, but sometimes, if experiences the most authentic may be trusted, from insights into the profound responsibilities of life which have been given to the dying, or to those who, having seemed to be the dying, have been called back to us again. Then, as the spirit was in act to step outward from its shaken tent (so it has been affirmed, again and again, and by the least imaginative and emotional of mankind), the past has come, gathered into one consciousness, full upon the conscience. In the half-unveiled presence of the Master of life the account-abilities of life have possessed the being. A whole world of obligation, not realized, has sprung silent and sudden into view. Happy they who in such an hour can say, in the firmness of faith that their Examiner is at the same moment also their Redeemer. Truly they know that they need His redemption then.

What shall we say in conclusion to all these things? Humbly, thankfully, lovingly, we will first remember that the Master who will preside at the scrutiny is at the same time the Lord who loves us and gave Himself for us. To Him His unworthiest workman is unspeakably dear, with that love which springs un-bought in a Saviour's heart. He will never be harsh, He will never be unfair. He will forget no extenuation, He will have understood every difficulty. Nevertheless, His eyes will be quite open, and He will express His entire opinion upon what we have done through the body.

And His opinion will be followed, assuredly, by results which will somehow affect the experiences of the servant even in the world of light and immortality. So, in St. Paul's words just following, to which we shall soon come, literally rendered, 'we know the fear of the Lord'. We recognize, we realize, the sol-emnity of the prospect of that scrutiny. We recall it when we are tempted to misuse 'the body', to forget the responsibility we have with these lips, and eyes, and hands, and feet, and brain.

But our last thought, as we remember how the two verses stand connected, shall not, after all, be only one of 'fear'. Rather it shall be full of a bright 'ambition'—bright as the clouds of the day of His appearing. Delightful call, to use these bodies, in which we live and move so happily, so habitually, *for Him*, by His grace alone, that 'Well done, good and faithful' shall be the voice of the beloved Master when He holds His domestic court at the breaking of the Resurrection dawn.

Thee may I set at my right hand,
  Whose eyes mine inmost substance see,
And labour on at Thy command,
  And offer all my works to Thee.

Give me to bear Thy easy yoke,
  And every moment watch and pray,
And still to things eternal look,
  And hasten to Thy glorious day.

For Thee delightfully employ
  Whate'er Thy bounteous grace hath given,
And run my course with even joy,
  And closely walk with Thee to Heaven.

                              —*C. Wesley.*

Chapter viii

THE ATONEMENT AND ITS MYSTERY OF MERCY

2 Corinthians v. 11-21

IN the passage now before us the great cardinal truth of the Atonement, with its attendant mysteries of merciful remission, reconciliation, and justification are dealt with. But the Apostle approaches this vast subject by reference to his own life's mission in prospect of the Master's Domestic Tribunal, in solemn view of which he last left us.

Ver. 11. **So,** with this in view, this prospect of such sacred solemnity in the Master's presence, **knowing** thus **the awe due to the Lord,** possessed by the thought of His majestic scrutiny of our work, we are compelled on the one hand to prosecute our evangelism unweariedly, on the other to keep every motive open to God, **men we persuade** to believe and to obey, **while to God we stand ready displayed** (perfect) as single-hearted in our motive and our ambition for Him; **aye, and I hope that in your consciences too we stand thus displayed,** recognized as meaning nothing but God's glory and your good. Do not mistake us in that thought; we are not nervously seeking over again to ask you to believe in us; we are but reminding you of the grounds you have on which to turn to our detractors and say, 'Our

Ver. 12. first evangelists were men above suspicion in motive as in message'. **Yes,**[1] **we are not trying over again to substantiate our claim to your trust;**[2] **we are giving an occasion to you for exultation with regard to us,**[3] **that you may have a reply to those** who would come between us and you, teachers **who are** themselves **in the face,** in the look, **exulting,** loud in their glorification of a legal sanctity and its rigid purism—**and yet** ($\mu\dot\eta$) **not** exulting **in heart** at all; for *that* Gospel never makes glad with the Lord's true joy. Yes, our whole thought and action, even when we have to assert ourselves, is for the

---

[1] omit $\gamma\grave\alpha\rho$.

[2] iii. 1.

[3] $\dot\upsilon\pi\grave\epsilon\rho\ \dot\eta\mu\hat\omega\nu$—ut qui vobis omnino dediti simus (**as those who have been given over altogether to you**).

Ver. 13. Lord and for you. **Were we,** on past occasions, **beside our-selves,** as it seemed? Did we witness for the truth with an energy which seemed fanatical? **It was to God;** we were possessed by the sense of His glorious claims. **Are we** now **sane and sober** in our judgment? calmly writing, and reasoning, and explaining? It is not for our own fair fame; **it is to you;** the one thought is to help you to **a** firmer grasp on truth. And indeed it must be so with us; we have no alternative; **for the love of our** ($\tau o \hat{v}$) **Christ,** the love He showed us in His dying glory,[1] **shuts us up** to such an aim and such a life, **coming as we came** (aorist), when we learnt to know Him, **to this judgment, that**[2] **One on behalf of**[3] **all died,**[4] nothing less than *died,* pouring out His soul to an unutterable death; **then, by inference** ($\check{a}\rho a$), having regard to the purpose of that death, **the all** in question **died,**[5] in His death for them; they, as it were, in Him, went—though all painlessly—through Gethsemane and Golgotha and the darkness, and have exhausted[6] so their sentence. And now, the effect alike in law and love is that they live in and for their Deliverer; **He on behalf of all** thus **died, that the living ones,** the beings joined to Him[7] in atoning death and now therefore in resurrection-life,[8] **should no longer to themselves be living** ($\zeta \hat{\omega} \sigma \iota v$), now that their very being as the saved is due to Him, **but to Him who on their behalf did die—and rise.**

St. Paul has had much to say in earlier chapters on the power of the Indwelling Christ. Now in this great passage he deals with the great primary truth of which the Indwelling Christ is the counterpart, namely, The Atoning Christ, our satisfaction.

In the later verses of the section above we notice particularly the thrice repeated phrase—'one died *for all*', 'He died *for all*', 'which died *for them*' (vv. 14, 15). So it is in the familiar Authorized Version. In the Greek original the preposition used throughout is $\dot{v}\pi\acute{\epsilon}\rho$, and each time we have translated 'on behalf of'. These phrases indicate the truth of CHRIST FOR Us and mark the dominant theme of the passage.

---

[1] Ver. 15 $\dot{a}\pi\acute{\epsilon}\theta a\nu\epsilon\nu$.
[2] omit $\epsilon\dot{\iota}$.
[3] hic $\dot{v}\pi\grave{\epsilon}\rho$ proximum est $\tau\hat{\wp}$ $\dot{a}\nu\tau\acute{\iota}$ (**here** $\dot{v}\pi\grave{\epsilon}\rho$ **is almost equal to** $\dot{a}\nu\tau\acute{\iota}$).
[4] The position is emphatic.
[5] Representative.
[6] Cf. Rom. vi. 7, 8; Col. iii. 3.
[7] In gratia, pace, spe, *Christo* (**In grace, peace, hope—in Christ**).
[8] This is assumed. See Rom. vi.

Would we live a life of deepest self-abasement, of holy 'fear and trembling' as regards the sacred claims of the Father's will upon the child, but still a life of profound peace, in which life and death are, as for St. Paul of old, a dilemma of blessings (Phil. i. 23); a life whose keynote shall be, 'I know whom I have believed, and I am persuaded that He is able to keep what I have committed to Him against that day' (2 Tim. i. 12); a life whose end shall be a calm, joyful 'going home to the Lord' (2 Cor. v. 8), meekly certain of His acceptance, quite sure that the sins and unrighteousness of the *whole past*, of the *whole* course, shall indeed be 'remembered no more'? (Heb. x. 17). Then let it be said, but with profound conviction, that that life must base its certainties for Justification on CHRIST FOR US.

Yes, and we may add, this very same love of Christ '*for us*', 'on behalf of us', in dying 'for our sins', also 'constrains us'. We have translated this 'shuts us up', as though 'Christ for us' shuts out all worldly sounds, shutting us in to the marvellous eternal love of Christ for all for whom He died. Yes, 'constrains us' to active service, so that we can hear no other call.

In our own case—and here, surely, he rises for a while above local references, into the grandeur of the Gospel-work in itself—such thoughts compel us sweetly to a life-programme emancipated from mere earthly motives (κατὰ σάρκα). **So that we,** we speak for ourselves, **from henceforth,**[1] from this crisis of our union with Christ, **know no-one flesh-wise;**[2] we cannot view our fellow-men out of a spiritual light, as they and we are affected by the Lord and His work; **even if we have** by possibility hitherto **known Christ Himself flesh-wise,**[3] viewed Him as but a personage of religious history, a mere leader, a mere 'cause' for our advocacy and interest, **now we know Him so no longer;** we can view Him only as our Lord, our Life, our Way, our End, our All, Whose we are and for Whom we think and act alone.

Ver. 16.

---

[1] Posited as present.
[2] Sine respectu aeternitatis (**without any regard to eternity**).
[3] Sc. solum historicè, sub specie temporis (ut multi nunc) (**Sc. only historically, and appearing for a time, as with many now**).

Ver. 17. **And thus,** for our case is but an instance of universal facts, **whoever is in Christ,** joined to Him in covenant and in Life, through faith, in that case there is **a new creation;**[1] relations and conditions are divinely and miraculously reconstructed; **the original things,** the state of unrenewed nature, **passed away** when he was joined to the Lord; **lo they,** those things, that state,[2] has **become new;** with the newness of new birth, new heart, new life, new relations to God in Christ.

Let us consider briefly some of the implications of the new life 'in Christ' of which St. Paul is speaking. It will help us the better to understand what is in his mind here, and also its connexion with what follows.

To be 'in Christ', to be 'rooted in Him', is not merely to love Him, not merely (with reverence be it said) to be loved by Him, though this mutual love is a divine thing. No; it is more. It is to be so dealt with as that the Life of the Lord is the basis, as it were, of all that is indeed Life for eternity in the believer. He is our Life. Not we live, but Christ liveth in us. Our mysterious personality, indeed, is untouched, untouched for ever, by this great fact. But saving that, so deep in the union of Being, of Nature, of Life, of Power, that the infallible Word runs thus concerning the believer, and nothing less is the truth: 'Not I, but Christ liveth in me'.

But, in the light of Scripture, 'in Christ' is a phrase which imports further ideas besides that of communicated Life. It imports, among other things, communicated interest, privilege, and covenant standing. Never for a moment does the Gospel really forget the sacred claims of Law. 'The life of Jesus may be manifest', and in blissful degrees of outshining beauty and of internal truth, 'in the mortal flesh' (2 Cor. iv. 11), and yet the saint may be (and if his view of facts is a healthy one, he will be) just the very man to shrink, with his face in the dust, before the uncreated Light of the spiritual Law. Coming into its presence, consciously and as a sinner, though a regenerate

---

[1] Cf. Gal. vi. 15; Rev. xxi. 5.
[2] Omit πάντα.

and life-possessing sinner, he comes across ideas and demands of *another order* than those of birth, and life, and health, and growth, and the out-blooming of the flower of glory from the holy bud of the present indwelling of his Lord. He, the same person in whom these ideas are being realized, and who is indeed, in their sense, 'in Christ, and Christ in him', needs from another side to see and grasp an 'in-ness' of another sort, harmonious but not the same, coincident but not the same; the 'in-ness' of an interest in the one solitary Human Obedience (Rom. v. 19) that meets the vast requirements, positive and negative alike, of that holy Law. Not one moment of his life, regenerate or unregenerate, into which disobedience (of defect or excess) has entered, can face that Law unshielded, uncovered.

It is towards this aspect of the Gospel and of the new life 'in Christ' that the Apostle's thought gravitates.

Wonderful transition! But its cause is sufficient; our Gospel and Ver. 18. its power are entirely divine; not Pauline but Divine. **These things, all of them,** the whole of this mighty change, **have origin in our God,** in Him **who reconciled us to Himself,** brought us to a glorious amnesty at His feet, **by means of** Jesus **Christ,** given for our sins, that we might be righteously welcomed back, **and** then **gave us,** conferred on us as privilege and boon as well as trust, **the agency of the reconciliation,** the work of being its heralds and ex-Ver. 19. pounders to men. And what is our message as His agents? It is **to the effect** (ὡς ὅτι) **that God,** God Himself, **was,** throughout the process of Redemption, **in Christ,** working within the sphere of His Person and His sacrifice, **reconciling the world to Himself,** providing a sacred amnesty for the fallen race, and thus **not reckoning to them their transgressions,** in the sense of an universal reprieve and, for all who seek, an abundant welcome; **and** then, it is God who **deposited in us,**[1] lodged as it were in our very beings, as the thing for which we exist, **the message of the reconciliation.**

In these verses let us particularly notice the repeated verb καταλλάσσω, I reconcile, and the repeated noun καταλλαγή, reconciliation or atonement. It has been said that the word *Atonement*

---

[1] ἐν ἡμῖν Acts xiii. 15.

itself by its etymology, 'at-one-ment', reconciliation, indicates that the true work of the sufferings of Christ is such a bringing of God and man together as would be needed if the need of conciliation lay wholly on man's side. In this view, the difficulty lay wholly in man's unsubdued will; in God there has never been anything but pure benevolence, yearning for the alienated to see it and come, and asking no condition but such coming. But, on this theory, the Atonement resides in *whatever* Christ was or did, with a view to breaking down man's misconceptions of God. And thus Christ's death stands in no *unique* position in His work. On such a view 'at-one-ment' would be effected, for many minds, not by His Death, but by the self-sacrificing beneficence of His Life, including the mingled majesty and love of the miracles, or by the divine charm of His words.

But an inductive study of Scripture negatives such a view. For the Lord's *Death* stands there in a place mysteriously unique. And besides, the words 'atonement', 'reconciliation', in Scripture do not lend themselves to such applications. Usage is often a safer guide than etymology to the meaning of words. So it is with 'atone'. The word is used in the Old Testament to represent the Hebrew 'cover', in connexions sacrificial and propitiatory. In the New Testament (Rom. v. 11) it is used, in the Authorized Version, for the Greek καταλλαγή. That word, and its cognates, habitually point to the winning rather the pardon of an ⸍   ⸌ded King than the consent of the rebel to yield to His kindness.[1] Thus in the verses following 'be ye reconciled to God' (ver. 20*b* below) will mean not so much, 'bend your pride to His unalterable benevolence', as 'secure, while you can, His acceptance'; an acceptance connected (ver. 21 below) with the sufferings of His Son.

We believe that an impartial review of these elements, and of the whole manner of presentation of the Saviour's death, will tend to the conviction that the immediate necessary purpose of the blessed Death was propitiatory, expiatory; not the moral suasion of man, nor even the procurement for man of new spiritual

---

[1] See, for illustrations from *non-theological* passages, 1 Sam. xxix. 4, where the LXX has διαλλαγήσεται; Matt. v. 24; 1 Cor. vii. 11. See *Pearson On the Creed*, Article X.

power, but expiation as towards God. It was the *sine quâ non*, under a divine plan, in order to lodge in the Sufferer, being Man, being the Second Man, a *Merit*, such as divine Holiness, without which God would not be God, should recognize as capable of more than balancing the demerit, the guilt, of sin. In the recognition of that guilt in its mysterious greatness lies some approach to a solution of the mystery of such an Atonement. There, certainly, lies the true secret of sympathy and submission as regards the fact of it.

In conclusion the Apostle commends the infinite mercy of the Atonement to the sympathetic hearing and ready submission of all men, and seeks in measure to clarify its mystery.

Ver. 20.   **On Christ's behalf, then,** as His agents, **we are an embassy** to men; we are the exalted Messiah's representatives; **as our** (τοῦ) **God is appealing by us** to men.[1] **We are on Christ's behalf beseeching** (them), **'Get reconciled to our** (τῷ) **God'**; secure the amnesty, the welcome, the vastly more than pardon, coming Ver. 21.   to His feet in repentant trust. For indeed the provision is adequate, the ground sure, the issue glorious. **Him who was such that He knew not sin,** sin never entered for one moment the region of His personal experience, **Him—on our behalf—He made sin,** so charged Him, loaded Him, implicated Him, in an inscrutable reality, with man's sin that it was, for the purpose of Redemption, as if *He* were *it*; in order on the amazing other side, **that we might become,** might *ipso facto* be (read γενώμεθα), on coming to Him, **God's righteousness in Him;**[2] that we sinners, implicated in and joined to the Lord, might in a wonderful correspondence be dealt with as if we were the embodied righteousness of God, the thing which wholly corresponds to His law, and so wholly receives the smile and welcome of the Judge.

Libraries of discussion have been written on the atoning cross. But the penitent spirit, when it has had a real vision of itself, and of the Crucified, *knows* that in Him, accepted, trusted, welcomed, is the only, and the perfect, and the present, and the perpetual peace and life.

---

[1] omnibus hominibus (**to all men**).
[2] Mirum (**A wonder**).

ADDITIONAL NOTES

1. The passage (2 Cor. v. 11-21) is of the first importance for the apostolic doctrine of the Atonement in its vicarious aspect. Note that there is an obvious balance and antithesis between the sense in which the Lord was made sin, and that in which we are made righteousness. Compare further the use by St. Paul very frequently of δικαιοσύνη in its forensic sense. 'Oh, blessed exchange (ὦ τῆς γλυκείας ἀνταλλαγῆς)! Oh, unsearchable workmanship! Oh, incredible benefits! That so the iniquity of many should be hidden in One Righteous, and the righteousness of One should justify many iniquitous!'
—*Epistle to Diognetus* (cent. ii), ch. ix (quoted in the author's *Justifying Righteousness*, 1885).

2. καταλλαγή. . Rom. v. 11; xi. 15; 2 Cor. v. 18, 19 (only). Also once in the LXX, Isa. ix. 5, where it is simply exchange; and once in the Apocrypha, 2 Macc. v. 20, where it is used in the New Testament sense. The verb καταλάσσω is also found in Rom. v. 10 *bis*; 1 Cor. vii. 11; 2 Cor. v. 18, 19, 20 (only). Note the extraordinary weight in the present passage. The primary meaning is the restoration of the favour of God to sinners who repent and put their trust in the expiatory death of Christ. Our laying aside of enmity is the secondary meaning. 'All attempts to make this secondary to be indeed the primary meaning and intention of the word, rest not on an unprejudiced exegesis, but on a foregone determination to get rid of the reality of God's anger against sin.'
—Trench, *Synonyms of the New Testament*, § lxxvii, q.v..

Chapter ix

THE DIVINE INHABITATION IN THE SAINTS—A STIMULUS TO PRESENT HOLINESS AND THE GOAL OF HOPE

2 Corinthians vi. 1-vii. 1

ST. PAUL has explained the wonderful provision, for our reconciliation, in order to our holiness; that holiness which never can be realized in the unreconciled, for it postulates harmony of relations with God in order to develop harmony of condition. And in the work of its proclamation and application he and those to whom he writes have the high privilege of being God's own collaborators, in the sense of being His faithful agents of evangelism. As such he now appeals to the as yet unreconciled to come and receive the gracious welcome.

Ver. 1. **But** (δὲ) **as** such **collaborators we appeal also** (καὶ) **to you** (ὑμᾶς emphatic) who *have* received it to go on to the development of peace in purity; we appeal to you **not to receive it in vain** (εἰς κενὸν cf. Gal. ii. 2; Phil. ii. 16; 1 Thess. iii. 5) so that the reception should end in nothing, should be futile, should be a deep final disappointment, **this** wonderful **grace of God** (cf. Rom. iii. 24; v. 2, 15, 20; vi. 1, 14; Gal. ii. 21; Eph. ii. 5), the welcome of the guilty into peace for the sake of the atoning Saviour; that free grace which is the glory of this age of the Gospel. **For** so **He says** in the Scripture

Ver. 2. (Isaiah xlix. 8) **'At a time accepted I hearkened to thee'** appealing sinner; **'and in salvation's day I rescued thee'**; and that means our period, the Gospel dispensation; **lo, now is that time graciously accepted,** (εὐπρόσδεκτος) **lo, now is salvation's day.** I return upon that thought, to remind you of the grand presentness of your freedom from the load of guilt, which the new teachers would postpone till I know not when. So we appeal to you to follow on from peace to

Ver. 3. holiness; and we seek to back our appeal with the example of a devoted life; **as those who present,** so far as they long and aim to do, **no stumbling block** to our converts **in anything, so that**

Ver. 4.   **our agency** as the Lord's messengers **may not be disgraced** by legitimate fault found with us. **No** (ἀλλά); **in everything we seek to substantiate our genuineness, as God's agents** (n.b. nominative) should do; with the substantiation of act and character, **in**

Ver. 5.   **large endurance under difficulty, in tribulations, in privations** (ἔσται γὰρ ἀνάγκη μεγάλη ἐπὶ τῆς γῆς, Luke xxi. 23), **in straits, in blows, in prisons** (cf. Matt. xiv. 10 of the Baptist, and Acts v. 19), **in riots** (ἀκαταστασίαις cf. Luke xxi. 9), **in toils, in sleepless nights, in lack of food**—no ceremonial is in view: and then, amidst all

Ver. 6.   these evidencing circumstances, we do it in the evidencing spirit, **in purity** of act, tone, talk, purity of morals, purity of aim (*verbum rarissimum* ἁγνότης) **in knowledge,** the manifestation of spiritual insight, the 'tongue of the taught, speaking in season' (Isaiah l. 4), **in patience** under provocation, 'the self-restraint which does not hastily retaliate a wrong' (Lightfoot), **in kindliness** of spirit and bearing, **in the Holy Ghost,** as His presence is evidenced—normal or abnormal— by results of blessing through weak but faithful agents, **in love un-**

Ver. 7.   **dissembled,** found out to be genuine by the thousand tests of life; **in word of truth,** as we speak a message verified by the awakened conscience and converted soul, **in God's power,** shown by conquests which no personnel of ours can account for; aye **and by our weapons** (see x. 4) **of true** (τῆς) **righteousness, for the right and for the left,** as we march and work along, beset on either hand, and utterly decline all dubious means of winning, using only the weapons of 'the light' (Rom. xiii. 12); by every various experience, used each as an

Ver. 8.   occasion for witness; **by glory and shame, by abuse and eulogy** (Lystra); the while our characters, by the mercy of God, are found to bear scrutiny, for we are reputed **as deceivers,**

Ver. 9.   **and true men,** according as we are 'found out', **as people to be ignored, and to be recognized,** society turning its back upon us, and yet involuntarily watching and seeing our true character, **as men dying,** for they are always saying it will soon be over with us and our cause, **and lo, we are alive,** hoping, working, winning still in Another's power; **as men under correction,** a Father's discipline

Ver. 10.   in trial, **and not done to death,** as by His judgment-stroke, **as men in pain, but always gladsome,** sensitive as human beings to sorrow, happy as believers in the will of God in it all; **as beggared, but enriching many,** mendicants as to earthly wealth, but filling hearts innumerable with the gold of grace; **as having nothing** (however abstract and hypothetical (μή)) **and yet grasping all things** with a possessor's hands, for all is ours in Christ (cf. 1 Cor. iii. 22, 23; vi. 19).

'We may take note here quite briefly of the grounds of the Apostle's appeal. First there is the thought that the time of grace is limited. St. Paul quotes from Isaiah—'I have heard thee in a time accepted, and in the day of salvation have I succoured thee'. Then comes the earnest affectionateness of his own ministry. He appeals on the ground of the work of Christ, and on the ground of those who were co-operators with Christ. 'We, then, as workers together with Him, beseech you'. This appeal is followed up by an account of his conduct as a fellow-worker; which again is succeeded by that glorious and touching description of ministerial devotedness which no Christian can read without humiliation. It was the unexaggerated picture of a human life actually lived out in this selfish world of ours. Note further that the grounds of apostleship alleged here are all spiritual; none are external. Thus St. Paul does not graft his right of appeal on any proud, priestly assumption, but on an inward likeness to Christ.'[1]

What an outburst! We could not refrain. The thought of our glorious message, and the thought of you so unutterably dear to us, has led us thus to pour out words about our ministry and its living credentials; if we may thereby more than ever endear and enforce the Gospel of present peace and God-given holiness in your hearts. Aye, **our mouth is open**
Ver. 11.   **towards you,** dear **Corinthians; our heart is expanded,** to take you all in afresh, and give you all our affection can give. **You are not straitened in respect of us;** your sense of some-
Ver. 12.   thing lacking, something that withstands your joy and power, has nothing to do with us, as if our commission was uncertain, our devotion to you lukewarm, or our message a mistake; **you are straitened in respect of your own hearts** (σπλάγχνοις), which have been distorted, and as it were shrunken, by this miserable false Gospel
Ver. 13.   so that you are afraid to take us and our message in. **Now so as to effect the same requital** do you do what we do, and that will be a rewarding requital to us, **I am speaking as Father to children;** it is a requital not of pay but of love that I mean; **do you too get expanded,** till you *can* take us and our message in.

Here the Apostle begins a fresh paragraph. However, it is not altogether separated from the words which have gone before.

---

[1] Non fastu sacerdotali, sed laboribus et patientia (**not by priestly arrogance, but by labours and by patience**).

And now, for one special and solemn application of our appeal to you to trust and obey us; one grand hindrance to your happiness is compromise with the evil world. From that we call you off, in the name not only of the Law but of this great Gospel of grace and promise.

Ver. 14. **Do not get to be wearers of an unequal yoke with unbelievers;**[1] engaging in connexions (e.g. marriage) where spiritual sympathy is impossible. **For what partnership is possible for righteousness and illegality? Or what communion is possible**
Ver. 15. **for light with darkness? What concord** (compact, agreement, compromise) **is possible for Christ with Belial,**[2] the Christian's holy Lord with His and our great enemy? **Or what part and lot has believer with unbeliever? Aye, what under-**
Ver. 16. **standing is possible for God's temple with idols? For we,** we Christians in our union in the Lord, **are the temple of God, the living God; as said our God** (of old) in many voices of His prophets, Moses, Isaiah, Jeremiah, Ezekiel, Zechariah, **'I will dwell in them, as my abode, and will walk in them,** as my haunt; **and I will be their God,** in the inmost sense of covenant union, **and they shall be my** chosen **people'.**

St. Paul is quoting here; he introduces the words with 'As God hath said'. For him, indeed, as for his Lord before him, the spiritual messages of the Old Testament are the very Word of God, through whatever human messenger they might come. As a fact, he is using here more than one such message, and blending them all into one. He takes one clause from Exodus, and another from Leviticus, and, in the immediate sequel goes on to Jeremiah, and Ezekiel, and Zechariah. But all alike is one thing as to its ultimate origin. It is, 'as God hath said'.

Come, let us read our treasure over again. 'I will dwell in them, and walk in them'. Such is the promise of the God of grace to the community of His faithful ones. Such, surely, is the promise also to the faithful member of that community, to the Christian who watches, prays, believes, obeys. Few are those promises to the Church which have not also their assured reference to the individual disciple's soul.

'I will dwell in them'. It is a wonderful word, when we take

---

[1] τὰ κτήνη σου οὐ κατοχεύσεις ἑτεροζύγῳ. Levit. xix. 19.
[2] Belial, probably, either Worthlessness or Perdition.

it aside and look at it anew in the light. Here is 'the high and lofty One, that inhabiteth eternity'. He is the sovereign Cause and Basis of existence. The universe is large. But relatively to HIM, in order and mode of being, it is 'a very little thing'. The persons alluded to in the promise are inhabitants of a sand-grain on the seashore of His vast creation. Moreover, they are beings who have misused a mysterious moral and personal relation to Him so as to turn away from Him, and sin. Nevertheless, they are so much to the eternal Heart (for the First Cause is also the eternal Heart) that, coming to bless them, He cannot say less than this, 'I will dwell in them'. Would it not be enough that He should pass them by on the roadside of the universe, and command His angels to spare and to tend them, while He is absent in greater scenes? Nay, He selects them for His personal abode. He is to be in residence and keep His court in them. 'I will dwell in them'.

Does the reader need to be reminded how full the whole Scripture is of that surprising promise? Let him read again Isaiah lvii, and John xiv, and Ephesians iii, and Revelation iii and xxi, and then explore the parallels they suggest. Let him follow up the study with an act of definite faith and appropriation; receiving afresh, and for deeper effects, the indwelling of his God.

But now the promise proceeds, and borrows from Leviticus this beautiful addition, 'I will walk in them'. What has this to say to the disciple's heart, in a special message of its own?

It indicates on the one hand, under striking imagery, the delight and repose of the gracious Indweller, His being indeed at home in his abode. On the other hand it has a precious intimation for the disciple as to what his Lord looks for in the heart-welcome given Him there.

'I will walk in them'. We seem to see the King in His mansion and its gardens. He is not merely there; He is there possessing and enjoying. At His will, at His leisure, He traverses the chambers, He surveys the points of view, He paces the alleys and the lawns. The place is His dear haunt, in which He 'lives and moves'. Oh, what benedictions to that 'haunt' are conveyed by that traversing Presence!

'I will walk in them'. Yes, and therefore to Him every gate
and avenue must be perpetually open. What would the lord of
some fair demesne say if he was constantly barred and hindered
in his home-walks by doors which his own servants had carelessly
left locked against him? Alas, the King eternal, who thus mysteriously delights to make room for His own abode in His creature's
heart, too often, by our grievous fault, finds it so. This chamber
and that, a department of the will, of the affections, of the imagin-
ation, is not quite open to Him today. Neglect, unprayerfulness,
self-indulgence, have left it locked; sin is in that corner, using
it for itself. But it belongs to the King! And He is in residence!
And hark, His step is at the door!

Lord, in Thy name we will keep the avenues open. Be pleased
to walk in them all, and haunt the whole place with Thyself.

Ver. 17. **Wherefore—'Come out from the midst of them,'** my true
Israel from the World's Babylon, **'and separate yourselves'**
from complexity with its sins, **saith the Lord, 'and unclean thing
touch ye not** (contrast Col. ii. 21). **And I will welcome you to
myself, and will be to you for Father, and you shall be
Ver. 18. to me for sons and daughters',** saith the Lord Almighty;
yes, the idea shall be realized, the titles shall become possessions, the
names facts.

Listen, not to threatenings now but to promises, and surrender your-
Ch. vii. 1 selves for holiness to their power. **Having then** (acting,
having, not needing to invent) **these as our promises,[1]
beloved ones,** let us—for here we put ourselves just at your side: the
word is for us all, always—**let us cleanse ourselves** in the believing
use of them so as to be free **from all pollution of flesh and spirit,**
alike in the world of sense and in that of thought, let us, by a decisive
act (aorist), set ourselves that way; so shall we be rightly placed for the
resulting process, **carrying towards its perfection sanctity in God's
fear.**

'*Having* therefore these promises, dearly beloved, let us cleanse
ourselves from all filthiness of the flesh and of the spirit' (2 Cor.
vii. 1); and '*Having* boldness to enter into the Holiest, by the

---

[1] Potentia promissionum. Magna vis est promissionum (**Potent promises.
Great is the power of the promises**).

blood of Jesus, let us draw near with a true heart, in full assurance of faith' (Heb. x. 19; and '*He that hath* the Son hath the life' (1 John v. 12).

What is the message of this class of passages, this rich and beautiful wealth of jewels of the Word, strung on this golden thread, 'we have'? It is that there is a large and all-important place in our Christian life for the use of humble but most positive assertion of our possessions. There is, indeed, and must be to the end, ample room for the soul's aspirations and petitions, its search and effort after things yet unattained. But even for these exercises of the spiritual life it is all important that we, if we are Christians indeed, if we have really come to the Lord in our need, to touch Him, and to live by Him, should never forget the right sort of assertion of the possessions which we have.

If I do not mistake, many a time of secret devotion would immensely gain in power and blessing by more recollection of this. Have we ever been conscious, at such moments, of a certain weariness and disappointment, in the use, perhaps of a familiar series of earnest petitions? Let us not give up petitioning; God forbid. Are not some of the very greatest promises which 'we have' linked to the precept 'ask'? But then 'we have' the promises. And often and again our petitioning would proceed with a new and delightful life and expectation if we would lay it aside for a while in order to re-affirm to ourselves what the promises are, and to re-affirm further to ourselves not only that they are, but that 'we have' them. Once at the feet of Jesus, once having touched, with fingers however cold and trembling, the hem of His garment (are not His promises His robe, for our touch by faith?), we have indeed boundless mercies still to ask. But we have at once one supreme mercy to give thanks for, because it is possessed, because 'we have' it. It is the mercy of Himself for us.

Is there one reader of these words who dares not yet say that he has 'touched the hem'? Yet for you also it is possible to use this talisman, 'we have'. You, too, 'have' at least one radiant promise for your own; '*Him that cometh unto Me I will in no wise cast out*'.

Chapter x

A RETROSPECT AND REVIEW

AT the point we have now reached an absolute pause appears in the Apostle's message. With Ch. vii. 1 closes what we may call the first part of the Epistle; a part, indeed, which again has to be sub-divided, and which is often interspersed with elements akin to the after second part, but which has on the whole a distinct character of its own. Broadly speaking Chs. i-vi are a series of statements of some of the highest and most spiritual aspects of Christian truth. We hardly need recall that they discourse *inter alia* upon the power of Divine παράκλησις in acute trial (Ch. i), upon the infinitely important issues of reception or rejection of the Gospel (Ch. ii), upon the contents and supreme significance of the New Covenant of the Spirit (Ch. iii) in its contrast with the Elder Covenant of the Letter, that is of the written Edicts of the Law; and of the power upon Christian workers of a present Indwelling of Christ and of the prospect, even immediately on death, of the enjoyment of His immediate presence (Chs. iv, v); of the prospect of the great *judicium domesticum* which He will hold when His servants are called to His tribunal to show their record of service (Ch. v); of the new creation; of the Atonement and its mystery of mercy (Ch. v); lastly, of the divine Inhabitation in the Saints, being alike the stimulus to an expectation of present holiness and the goal of hope, as the obedient Christian increasingly realizes its blessings (Ch. vi). All these supremely important topics illuminate the first chapters, and will always make 2 Corinthians an inestimable field of spiritual study, as long as the Church is true to her faith that the written Scriptures are indeed the Word of God, and not merely the thinking of man.[1]

We must not forget meanwhile that these great treasures of truth are imbedded, or rather embodied, for the whole structure of the Epistle is a living organism, in matter which is intensely

---

[1] Consult Appendix C.1(d), second paragraph, p. 144.

personal, local, and occasional. It will be an instructive study to take Chs. i-vii. 1, and read them over from *this* point of view. We shall then see with fresh interest how paragraphs which reveal to us the highest spiritual facts and prospects spring quite naturally out of remarks or reflections on the writer's relations with Corinth, with particular persons or parties at Corinth, or out of the general experience of his labours and sufferings. For example, the noble assertion (i. 19, 20) that Christ is the great Yea introducing the promises and Amen closing them, springs direct from the incident of St. Paul's own change of plans as regards his intended visit to Corinth and from the charge of fickleness which it had occasioned. The grand statement of the essence of the apostolic Gospel in Ch. iv appears to spring from a reminiscence just then and there of the poor shifty would-be Gospel which his opponents were trying to plant at Corinth. His ever memorable assertion of the Christian's immediate blessedness at death, seeing the Lord, arises from his remarks upon his own labour as an apostle, and these are made not in respect of nothing, but in view of the accusation which certain persons were spreading at Corinth about him. Lastly, the noble recitation of the Old Testament promises about JEHOVAH's Habitation and Haunt (ἐμπεριπατήσω) in His saints is given not without a close reference to local context. It is occasioned by his anxious consciousness of social and religious compromises at Corinth, in marriage and otherwise, which would so grievously impede the personal advance of the converts in Christian holiness.

A review of these first six chapters on such a line will, I hope, greatly aid in the realization of that grand character of so very large a part of Scripture, its combination of the occasional and the eternal. Continually we find it so busy with things of the place and the hour that we may study it, from one side, with an interest altogether like that we bestow on a purely secular writing; and it will exercise our intelligence to a high degree in so doing. But we shall also continually find it developing these local and temporal elements into revelations of eternal and undiscoverable truths, infinitely precious. Few Scriptures are more illustrative of such a remark than 2 Corinthians.

After these observations we may refer to that masterly book, Canon T. D. Bernard's *The Progress of Doctrine in the New Testament*, for the value of the Epistolary form of so much Christian Revelation. A full extract will prove none too long. The passage is introduced by an enquiry into the place and function of the apostolic Epistles ('the Apostle', as the Fathers often call them collectively) in the plan of Revelation. Attention is drawn to the evidence given by our Lord's words, and by the nature of the case, to the divine *intention* that the Apostles should develop and complete the personal teaching of their Master; were it otherwise we should (probably) have to face the riddle of a delivery of doctrine by Christ which assumed, which promised, a sequel and completion, but never received it. Accordingly we are right to read the Epistles with the same reverent confidence which we bring to the Gospels and their Discourses; they are equally, and with a profound purpose, the message of the King.

Canon Bernard proceeds:

'The Lord recognized this necessity. He met it by the living voice of His Apostles; and their Epistles remain as the permanent record of this part of their work. They are the voice of the Spirit, speaking within the Church to those who are themselves within it, certifying to them the true interpretations and applications of the principles of thought and life which as believers in Jesus they have received. . . . The *form* in which this teaching is given to us is very significant. "The epistolary form," says Bengel, "is a pre-eminence of the Scriptures of the New Testament as compared with those of the Old". It is a suggestive remark, reminding us of that open communication and equal participation of revealed truth which is the prerogative of the later above the former dispensation; indicating, too, that the teacher and the taught are placed on one common level in the fellowship of truth. The Prophets delivered *oracles to the people*, but the Apostles wrote *letters to the brethren*, letters characterized by all that fullness of unreserved explanation, and that play of various feeling, which are proper to that form of intercourse. It is in its nature a more familiar communication between those who are, or should be, equals. That character may less obviously force upon us the sense, that the light which is thrown on all subjects is that of a divine inspiration; but this is only the natural effect of the greater fullness of that light; for so the moonbeams fix the eye upon themselves, as they burst through the rifts of rolling clouds, catching the edges of objects, and falling on patches of the landscape; while under the settled brightness of the genial and universal day, it is not so much the light that we think of as the varied scene which it shows.

'But that the fact that the teaching of the Apostles is represented by their *letters*, is a peculiarity, not only in comparison with the teaching of the Prophets, but with ancient teaching in general, which is perpetuated either in regular treatizes or conversations preserved in writing. The form adopted in the New Testament combines the advantages of the treatize and the conversation. The letter may treat important subjects with accuracy and fullness, but it will do so in immediate connexion with actual life. It is written to meet an occasion. It is addressed to particular states of mind. It breathes the heart of the writer. In these respects it suits well with a period of instruction in which the Word of God is to be given to men, not so much in the way of information as in the way of *education*; or, in other words, in which the truth is to be delivered, not abstractedly, but with a close relation to the condition of mind of its recipients.

'Thus it is delivered in the Epistles. Christ has been received; Christian life has been commenced; Christian communities have been formed; and men's minds have been at work on the great principles which they have embraced. Some of these principles in one place, and others of them in another, have been imperfectly grasped, or positively perverted, or practically misapplied, so as to call for explanation or correction; or else they have been both apprehended and applied so worthily, that the teacher . . . feels able to open out the mysteries of God. . . . These conditions of mind were not individual accidents. Rome, Corinth, Galatia, Ephesus, supplied examples of different tendencies of the human mind in connexion with the principles of the Gospel—tendencies which would ever recur, and on which it was requisite for the future guidance of the Church that the Word of God should pronounce. It did pronounce in the most effectual way, by those letters which are addressed by the commissioners of Christ, not to possible but to actual cases, with that largeness of view which belongs to spectators at a certain distance from the scene, and with that closeness of application which personal acquaintance dictates and personal affection inspires'.

A little further on, Canon Bernard speaks of the *method* of apostolic teaching, as in perfect harmony with this its *form*. 'It is a method of companionship rather than of dictation. The writer does not announce a series of revelations, or arrest the enquiries which he encounters in men's hearts by the unanswerable formula, "Thus saith the Lord". He . . . utters his own convictions, he pours forth his own experience, he appeals to others to "judge what he says", and commends his words "to their conscience in the sight of God". He confutes by argument rather than by authority. . . . Such a method necessarily creates a multitude of occasions for hesitation or objection; and it has been proposed to meet these difficulties by the principle that we are bound to accept the conclusions as matters of revelation, but not to assent to the validity of the arguments or the applicability of the quotations. The more we enter into the spirit of the particular passages which have been thought to require that qualification, the more we feel that it can only have seemed necessary, from a want of real and deep harmony with the mind of Scripture'.

The extract is long; the temptation was to make it longer, so valuable is the whole context. What has been quoted will surely be felt to be altogether to the point as we address ourselves to the study not only of an Epistle but of this Epistle, so entirely full of the personality and sympathies of the writer, and with such close and tender application for the realities of human life and Christian service.[1]

---

[1] For further extracts see Extended Note—*Coalescent Inspiration*, p. 161.

But we come, now, to the latter half of the Epistle, and we shall find here a certain difference. It is a difference not in the character of the elements of the writing but in their adjustment and proportion. The personal, local, occasional comes very much more to the front; the direct revelational statements are less frequent and full. Not that the writing is less Holy Scripture, or less truly θεόπνευστος. But the θεοπνευστία takes a different line of action. It speaks to us more through Saint Paul's personality than before. But it equally speaks to us from Jesus Christ and to convey His mind.

We shall find this second half of the Epistle falling naturally into two sub-divisions. The first is Chs. vii, viii, ix, in which reference is made first to the recent circumstances of trial and sorrow in the mission, most affectionately dealt with, and then to the great enterprise of the collection for the Jerusalem poor, so near St. Paul's heart, as a loving finale to his work in the Eastern Mediterranean; when again he refers with the kindliest and most delicate appreciation to the rivalry in good works of the Macedonian and Achaian missions. Then we have Chs. x, xi, xii, xiii, which have been treated by some critics as a separate document, a Four-Chapter-Letter, *Vierkapitelbrief*—and identified with the letter alluded to vii. 8, which he almost wished he had never written. Those chapters are a grave, stern indictment upon certain whom he recognizes as embittered and unscrupulous opponents, and most dangerous misrepresenters of the Lord's message. He is forced to denounce them, even to satirize them, and to close with words of sorrowful gravity about his approaching visit to Corinth, in view of the situation they have created.[1]

In the persons thus attacked we shall see, surely unmistakably, leaders of that Judaistic party which everywhere (since Acts xv) seems to have followed St. Paul about. The troubles at Corinth from rivalries and divisions seem to have modified their shape considerably between 1 Corinthians and 2 Corinthians.[2] When 1 Corinthians was written there were many divergent streams of thought or of personal preference; the parties or cliques of Apollos,

---

[1] See further pp. 96, 97; Appendix D 1, p. 155.
[2] See *Introduction*, Sec. ix, p. xxix.

Cephas, Paul and Christ. When 2 Corinthians was written it would seem that the latter tendency with its curious title οἱ Χριστοῦ (Christ's party) was alone prominent in the field. Its leaders, we may fairly infer, found a peculiar opportunity in (1) the no doubt sadly disorganized and even demoralized tone of Corinthian Christian life in many cases, giving occasion to say, 'See what this so-called free-grace Gospel bears as its fruits', and (2) in the line of action taken by St. Paul, which at first no doubt might be mistaken for weakness, and would as such tempt an unscrupulous party of determined opponents to do their worst, and to rouse the impression that he was all the while conscious that he was no genuine Apostle at all, and dared not act as such.

But it is time to come again to our text itself. We shall find St. Paul, after his just-uttered call to the Corinthians to lead the true Christian life, turning to them with a purely personal appeal to see in him again just their spiritual father and friend, unaltered, unalterable, and with his likeminded helpers, longing for their blessing.

Chapter xi

RECENT CIRCUMSTANCES OF TRIAL AND SORROW IN THE MISSION

2 Corinthians vii. 2-16

As we have already observed, at this point in the epistle there is a complete pause. Perhaps the Apostle had left Philippi and was now nearer to Thessalonica and therefore nearer to Corinth. Titus' presence, moreover, as a visible link with Corinth would be calculated to induce him to give his attention to those practical problems which would confront him on arrival. At any rate, we note that when Paul dictates again he is concerned in the main, and more and more so as the letter proceeds, with those matters which are more exclusively local and occasional, the kind of practical concerns which would engage his attention on arrival at Corinth.

The Apostle begins by resuming his previous appeal Ch. vi. 11-13.

Ver. 2. [1]**Make room for us** in your hearts,[2] as we have just told you (vi. 11) our heart is enlarged to take you in: **not a man did we injure,** in person, property, or name, in all that past intercourse with you; **not a man did we corrupt,** in principle or morals; **not a man did we overreach**[3] by false teaching for interests of our own.[4]

Ver. 3. **With no wish to condemn you** (πρὸς κατάκρισιν), as if I was your judge, or your master, am I speaking (n.b. singular) in all these appeals to you, and warnings, and reproofs; **for I have already**

---

[1] Pericope prorsus nova (**On to a new paragraph**).

[2] So R.V.M. and Segond's French—Donnez-nous une place dans vos coeurs (**Give us a place in your hearts**). (*La Sainte Bible, qui comprend l'Ancien et le Nouveau Testament, traduits sur les textes originaux hébreu et grec, par Louis Segond.* Imprimerie de l'Université: Oxford, 1880. This translation is used in the second half of the Epistle, and afterwards referred to simply as Segond. See Appendix C, Sec. 1(d), third paragraph and footnote, p. 145.)

[3] See the same word, xii. 17, 18.

[4] felices illi (**how good for them**).

said[1] that in our very hearts you are, aye, to die with you and to
live with you; yours is a place in our affections which makes it our
delight to be identified with you in every possible experience.[2]

These verses seem to retain a lingering echo of one of the
deepest notes of the earlier part of the epistle, especially in Ch.
iv. There he had said, 'So then death worketh in us, but life in
you' (iv. 12), and the words epitomize God's message to them
through his own affliction. Here in Ch. vii he touches again on
a similar theme. 'Ye are in our hearts to die together and to live
together'. In the next verse he refers once more to his tribulation
and then passes on to the chief subject of the chapter, namely,
the arrival of Titus, which was a tonic to him, and a signal that
matters were improving as between him and his dearly loved
converts in Corinth.

'The end of a quarrel between friends is like the passing away
of a storm; the elements are meant to be at peace with each other,
and nature never looks so lovely as in the clear shining after rain.
The effusion of feeling in this passage, so affectionate and unreserved; the sense that the storm clouds have no more than left
the sky, yet that fair weather has begun, make it conspicuously
beautiful even in the writings of St. Paul.'

Ver. 4.   **Great indeed is my outspokenness towards you; yes, I**
admit I have written with all the freedom possible in warning
and appeal; but then, equally, if you could but hear it, **great is my
exultation over you.** Such are you to me that the least encouragement
from Corinth, the least news of your spiritual prosperity, or restored
internal union, or rising liberality is bliss to me; **I stand full to the brim
with such encouragement, I am running over the brim with such
joy, aye, on the top of all our tribulation;**[3] though that tribulation is
there all the time, underlying the circumstances; the joy runs over it.

---

[1] Perhaps vi. 11.
[2] mira Evangelii sympathia (**wonderful fellow feeling in the cause of
the Gospel**).
[3] For the construction cf. i. 4, ὁ παρακαλῶν ἡμᾶς ἐπὶ πάσῃ τῇ θλίψει. Here the
R.V. has 'in all our affliction': Segond 'au milieu de' (**in the middle of**). He is,
as it were, taking that tribulation as the ground on which to pour the joy.
Mira verba (**wonderful words**).

Let me explain myself by telling you what has lately happened.

Ver. 5.   **For on our coming into Macedonia,** from the Troad (ii. 12, 13), **our flesh,** our natural feelings apart from the grace of God[1], **had[2] no relief,** no rest from tension[3] (cf. 2 Thess. i. 7): **no** (ἀλλά); **troubled[4] in every respect; outside, battles, inside, fears.**

Ver. 6.   Such was the position, the θλίψις, which so wonderfully counteracted through good news of you; as thus. **But the encourager of the lowly** (R.V.), the depressed, the low-laid,[5] **our** (ὁ) **God, encouraged us[6] through[7] the arrival** (παρουσία) **of Titus,**[8] fresh from his visit

Ver. 7.   at our instance to you (following on the First Epistle). To see him, merely as a relief to the tension of silence, was a great comfort; so through his mere arrival we were cheered; **but not only through his arrival; but through the encouragement with which he,** as we soon found, **was encouraged over you;** he was in the happiest mood about your attitude; **reporting[9] to us your yearning,[10]** the affectionate, wistful, missing wish for our re-visit, **your lamentation,**

---

[1] Compare the remarkable *other side* of the experience—ii. 13 οὐκ ἔσχηκα ἄνεσιν τῷ πνεύματί μου. His spirit felt the strain which pervaded his whole being in its sensibilities and emotions, and so also his flesh. σάρξ is the earthly nature of man apart from divine influence, and so prone to sin. Cf. xii. 7, σκόλοψ τῇ σαρκί.

[2] ἔσχηκεν—so read, though ἔσχεν has some support. So 2 Cor. ii. 13. Cf. Rev. v. 7, ἦλθε καὶ εἴληφεν; vii. 14, καὶ εἴρηκα αὐτῷ. In these latter we have surely cases where the tenses are not distinguished; the action cannot be said to be continued up to the present. (Aliter (**elsewhere**) probably Heb. xi. 17, 28, where permanent effects and impressions are in view). Perhaps even here in 2 Cor. vii. 5 we have a case of blending the distinction of the tenses, though just possibly it is a vivid presentation.

[3] Ah combien! (**O how great!**).

[4] A free loose use of the participle is characteristic of St. Paul, cf. Rom. xii. 9, 14, 15, 16. The rendering above is left as literal as possible, to convey the vivid naturalness of the style. We may, of course, paraphrase it—'It was a sense of nothing but difficulty and trial; open violence was around us, and in view of it we had very trembling hearts within'.

[5] καρδία ταπεινή, a discouraged heart. Ecclus. xxv. 23. ἅπαξ in New Testament in this sense; les abattus (**the cast down**)—Segond.

[6] AMEN! ita etiam hodie esse potest (**AMEN: so also can it be today**) (v. 5b and 6a).

[7] ἐν instrumenti (**instrumental** ἐν).

[8] ii. 13; also vii. 13, 14; viii. 6, 16, 23; xii. 18.

[9] ἀναγγέλλων often classicè for a messenger's report, cf. Acts xiv. 27, these 'reported' the incidents of the tour. In the New Testament it is often used less precisely for 'proclaim' or 'disclose', as the magicians at Ephesus, Acts xix. 18.

[10] See below ver. 11. Only here in New Testament and Biblical Greek except Ezekiel xxiii. 11 (Aquila). Cf. ἐπιποθεῖν, 2 Cor. v. 2; Rom. i. 11; Jas. iv. 5; Rom. xv. 23 (ἐπιποθία—ἅπαξ). Phil. iv. 1 (ἐπιπόθητος). The idea is much like a homesick yearning. Here it implies a wish for his presence—desiderium. (**a longing**).

your demonstrative sorrow[1] over the past, **your enthusiasm[2] over me** (n.b. the singular breaking in here); the rush of renewed personal attachment and gratitude, the loving jealousy for my injured reputation; **so that I rejoiced even more** than under the general impression that things were better; the bright details enhanced my delight. For let me tell you that this happiness was so peculiar because of my quite peculiar feeling over the letter which not so long ago you received from me, that letter in which I had felt constrained to speak with such urgency and pain.[3]

St. Paul has been, from vii. 2 onwards, pouring his heart out over the subject of the pains and joys, so closely connected, of his recent intercourse. That sad letter! The rush of conflicting feeling which followed it! The wish he had never sent it! Then the unspeakable relief of Titus' return, with such a report, and, best of all, such a beaming face! After all, the letter was God-guided; for it occasioned, by His grace, this revulsion to a better mind which had so delighted Titus.

Oh, that we could have read that letter! I more than suspect that, if we could do so, we should find that whatever stern, plain speaking it contained, it was warm all through with affection. The sternness was of the sort which is possible only when the writer cares so vastly much about the reader that he cannot help the utmost urgency of manner. No wonder that, when once God moved their hearts at all towards Himself again, such a letter should call forth not only repentance but 'enthusiasm for the writer'. We cannot now recover that letter. But by the way we may see a grand specimen of the sort of message it must have been, in the Epistle to the Galatians. Read it over, and can you not believe that about it also the mighty but sensitive heart of the Apostle could easily have been 'by way of wishing' he hadn't written it? Like other letter writers in painful correspondence he would, in a certain mood, vividly remember every wounding word, but would not so well remember how he had betrayed

---

[1] ὀδυρμός; Vulg. fletum (**weeping**). Segond, vos larmes (**your tears**). ἅπαξ in New Testament. 2 Macc. xi. 6 for the grief which cries and prays for a 'good angel'.

[2] ζῆλος: ζέω—excitement. A word capable of good or bad meaning; and so different from φθόνος.

[3] Ver. 7. Animus Apostoli perfectè humanus est (**The mind of the Apostle is perfectly human**).

intense interest and affection, too.   Can we not imagine the
Epistle to the Galatians likewise exciting a burst of ζῆλος?

Ver. 8.   **Because even if,** even though, **I did inflict pain on you in
the letter**[1] you know of, **I do not regret**[2] the writing of it
now, **though as a fact I was by way of regretting it** (n.b. the imperfect, cf. Rom. ix. 3); half wishing that it had never gone.   **For I see** at a
glance **that that letter, even though in passing** only, **did inflict pain**,
Ver. 9.   and of course this is in itself pain to me.   But **now,** under the
altered cicumstances of information, **I am happy, not that
you were put to pain, but that you were put to pain with the result
of repentance;**[3] it has been a pain that has issued in a spiritual revolution of thought and will.   **For you were put to pain after God's
manner,** under conditions ruled and blessed by Him, **in order that
you might get in no respect loss**[4] **by action of ours;** He so used
the verbal rebuke as to bring you, by moral conviction, compelled only
by conscience, to yourselves again;[5] and thus all need of harsh *action* on
our part was precluded, action which, however necessary, could not but
somehow inflict loss for the time upon the fullness and joy of your life.
Ver. 10.   **For the pain after God's sort,**[6] brought home by Him with
inward blessing, **works out repentance,** spiritual revolution,
resulting in salvation,[7] safety in Christ, attained or developed, **never
to be regretted; but the world's sort of pain,**[8] apart from grace,
the pain which means mere infliction without conviction, **works out** the
sad opposite of repentance, **death;** it tends to the death of conscience,
in the throes of wounded pride, and so ultimately to the soul's ruin.

---

[1] 1 Corinthians, and cf. 2 Thess. iii. 14.
[2] μεταμέλομαι is the lower word as compared with μετανοέω.   The present
passage illustrates this well.   Note carefully the relation between λύπη and
μετάνοια.   Perhaps only in Heb xii. 17 does μετάνοια mean other than spiritual
revolution.   μετάμελος, μεταμέλεια are classical.
[3] Vs. 8b and 9a—oratio fracta sua ipsius vehementia (sive potius suo ipsius
amore) (**his speech is broken by the strength of his own feelings, or
rather of his love**).
[4] μηδενὶ ζημιωθῆτε—pulchrum (**beautiful**).
[5] 'What is spiritual ministry?   It is that if you see me to be wrong you are
able by prayer, by spiritual power, by tact, by love, by forbearance and patience
to enlighten my conscience, and thus cause me gladly to turn from my mistaken
course to the right one'.   *Life of Hudson Taylor*, vol. ii. p. 582f.   The whole
incident from the mission field there recorded is a perfect illustration of St.
Paul's spiritual technique as revealed in this passage.—(Ed.).
[6] Petrus (**Peter**).
[7] σωτηρία—initial Luke xix. 9, John iv. 22 perhaps; medial Phil. i. 19, ii. 12;
final Rom. xiii. 11.
[8] Judas (**Judas**).

St. Paul is not disclosed in his writings or speeches as pre-eminently a preacher of repentance like the Baptist. He is rather concerned with setting forth Jesus Christ as the great Living Centre of the Kingdom of God. Apart from the present passage the word repentance only occurs in his writings in Rom. ii. 4, and 2 Tim. ii. 25. Yet in this passage now before us, although it contains no exact definition of the word, we have perhaps the best description of repentance to be found anywhere in Scripture. In the verse just paraphrased (ver. 10) he describes repentance as rising in godly sorrow. In the verse which follows (ver. 11) he describes it as issuing forth in earnest care, clearing of themselves, indignation, fear, longing, zeal and avenging.

God sees sin not in its consequences but in itself; a thing infinitely evil, even if the consequences were happiness to the guilty instead of misery. So sorrow, according to God, is to see sin as God sees it. The grief of Peter was as bitter as that of Judas. He went out and wept bitterly; how bitterly none can tell but they who have learned to look on sin as God does. But in Peter's grief there was an element of hope; and that sprang precisely from this—that he saw God in it all. Despair of self did not lead to despair of God.

It was from this 'pain after God's sort' that there flowed out the abundant river of repentance which St. Paul proceeds to describe, especially in reference to their relationship with himself and their attitude to his recent injunctions.

Ver. 11. Your pain, thank God, was of the right sort, evidenced by results. **For look now, this precise thing, this being put to pain** (aor.)[1] **in God's fashion,** under conditions chosen and blessed by Him, think what it did in you! **What an intense** ($\pi\acute{o}\sigma\eta\nu$) **earnestness**[2] it **wrought** in you, earnestness to set wrong right with all your hearts; **aye, and vindication** of your motives and conduct to the utmost possible, under consciousness of the extreme gravity of the charges, **and indignation**[3] against yourselves for the spirit of rivalry and disorder, **aye, and fear** of an aggrieved Lord, and even of His servant's

---

[1] omit ὑμᾶς.

[2] empressement (**eagerness**)—Segond.

[3] ἀγανάκτησις. The noun is ἅπαξ in New Testament. The verb is common in classical and New Testament Greek (only in the Gospels, e.g. Matt. xx. 24 over James and John).

further reproofs, **aye, and yearning** wish to have me back, aye, **aye, and enthusiasm** for my person and work, **aye, and avenging,** strong measures taken, or to be taken, in chastening obstinate offenders by your own action! Yes, **in every respect,** in your whole spirit and conduct, as Titus reported it, **you established your purity,** as to the present position, **in** (with regard to, if ἐν is omitted) **the matter;**[1] you made it clear that, as a Church, you are now singlehearted in your desire to do

Ver. 12.　absolutely right in respect of the recent troubles.[2] **So** when I look back on my stern letter, and on Titus' visit and his bright report, and interpret causes by effects I may even say of that letter that it was written, however little I saw it quite so at the time, on purpose to give you this opportunity for a more than recovery of a true attitude. Yes, **even though I did write to you** as I did, **it was not,** anyhow from God's point of view, **on account of**[3] **the injurer,** and simply because So-and-so had sinned against his fellow Christian, and needed to be put to shame, **nor on account of the injured one**[4], simply because So-and-so had been sinned against and must be righted; I do not mean that I was not seriously thinking of them, but that a deeper and higher aim lay concealed in my action, as guided by my Lord; **yes** (ἀλλά) **on account of,** with a view to, **your enthusiasm,** that which you feel **over us, thus being disclosed to your own view, in the presence of our** (τοῦ) **God.** That letter, as a fact, has brought you to a strong consciousness of your real sympathies and convictions; it has made you feel that 'your heart is in the right place' towards the truth and towards me, and this, 'in the sight of God', in a way connected with deep spiritual processes, His conviction of sin, His message of full salvation.

Ver. 13.　**For this reason,** recognizing divine blessing latent in most painful circumstances **we feel encouraged.**[5] **Yes, and** (δὲ: addition with slight modification) **on the top of our own encouragement,** as a crown upon it, gilding its gold, **with even greater effusion we rejoiced at the joy of Titus,** it was contagious to us, it was even better than his news, because it showed that your state was better than anything he could put in so many words; **because his spirit,** his inmost being, **abides refreshed** by the cheer he has derived **from all of you.**[6] So

---

[1] τῷ πράγματι, cf. 1 Thess. iv. 6.

[2] Ver. 11; fructus resipiscentiae (**the result of coming to their senses**).

[3] εἵνεκεν = ἕνεκεν = ἕνεκα.

[4] This *appears* to suggest a different occasion from 1 Cor. v. 1. It is, however, clear that it refers to the same as 2 Cor. ii. 5-11, where the masculine particles show that it was some case of grave scandal in which one man had done grievous wrong to another. Whether or no this was the wrong done by the man to his father (1 Cor. v), it is evident that the incident indicated in ii.5-11, and again here, was the incident to which he had referred in his supplementary letter.

[5] παρακεκλήμεθα: the perfect emphasizes the abiding and present consciousness

[6] suave! (**sweet!**).

profound is his relief, so happy his expectation, it is new life to him, and through him to us; for it is the most joyful possible vindication of

Ver. 14. my warm words about you to him before he started. **Because in any language of exultation over you which I have used to him, I was not put to shame**[1] when he came to personal intercourse with you; he found you all that I had described. So our veracity was proved all round; my message to you, my Gospel and then my warnings, were as a fact true, and now Titus sees that we have only said truth about you; I was not put to shame in his eyes; **rather** (ἀλλά), **just as we spoke everything to you in truth** when we were with you, and when we wrote to you, **so our exulting** language over you, **as**

Ver. 15. uttered **in Titus' presence**[2] before he set out, **turned out to be** just **truth.**[3] And now, so entirely is this so, so delighted is he with his experience, **his heart** (σπλάγχνα) **with growing effusion goes out to you, as he calls up,** thinks over in review, **your quite unanimous obedience** to our appeal through him; **how you received him**[4] when he came **with fear and trembling,**[5] with the humbled anxiety of those who are really convinced of sin and resolved to break with it altogether.

So to sum up my whole feeling—**I am happy because in everything**

Ver. 16. **I am full of courage,** I feel new strength and spirits in my whole field of labour, **in you** for reasons residing in your loyalty and love, your recovery of the right attitude towards the truth and me.[6]

Here closes the first strain, so to speak, of this section of the Epistle. Let us think of some of its exquisitely human characteristics, for indeed it is a passage which, however guided by

---

[1] κεκαύχημαι: the perfect implies that St. Paul stands to it still—'I have used and do use'. Though uttered before Titus went it was but the expression of his settled and so present feeling. κατῃσχύνθην is aorist as denoting a past incident.

[2] ἐπὶ Τίτου: a somewhat solemn phrase, frequently for courts of justice, as if Titus were to judge. 'Auprès de Tite' (**before Titus**)—Segond.

[3] Ver. 14, humanum (**human**).

[4] Titus fortis erat: Timotheus dulcis (**Titus was forceful: Timothy pleasing**).

[5] For φόβου καὶ τρόμου cf. 1 Cor. ii. 3; Eph. vi. 5; Phil. ii. 12, and see also Psalm ii. 11, 'Serve with fear, rejoice with trembling'. The meaning here is as little abject before man as in 1 Cor., Ephes., or Phil. It is the anxiety of one who feels his inability to meet all requests, but religiously does his utmost to fulfil his duty.

[6] O amicus et pastor (**O friend and shepherd**).

Heaven, lives and moves with the absolutely free and genuine emotion of a beating heart. Note one point among others; the subtle naturalness with which Paul, between ver. 2 and ver. 16, 'boxes the compass', we might almost say, in his feeling about the Corinthians. 'Make room for us in your hearts'; there is one side of the circle. He is conscious at that moment of the abiding presence, here and there in Corinth, in some minds, however few, of sentiments not quite trustful and cordial to him. Some such minds of course there were. The Judaists still had some following; and beyond their following they had made, of course, a certain impression; many a Paulist had been troubled by them, and he could not know how far this was so still with one and another. Thinking of that, he speaks as one who had to ask for a welcome, to entreat their confidence; and to protest his own true conduct; and to say how much he loves them, and how he praises them. Then we come on, by delicate steps of natural connexion, to the mention of Titus, and his coming. It is alluded to just to illustrate how dear Corinth is to him; it is adduced to show how good news from them can revolutionize every feeling for him. So he is drawn on into that particular reminiscence; he dwells on Titus' coming, he lives it over again; and now, in that light, his wistful heart passes from the darker side of Corinth to the splendidly bright side. He basks, as it were, in that pleasant glow. He recalls the report, so evidently good as a whole, brought by Titus. And its details, backed by the reporter's whole air and manner, so fill his heart that he can think of nothing else. He is another man, ready for anything, full of heart and hope, because of them. He is courageous for every trial now, and it is 'in them'. He says not a word of appeal for admission to their hearts. It is all well.

Shall we call this inconsistency? Surely not; it is but the depth and fullness of the human heart, moving with its mysterious life. It is as little inconsistent as the tides. It is the absolutely truthful expression of absolutely natural experiences. If those experiences are in some degree conditioned by our finite limits, if they show that even a St. Paul could not see all sides of a position at the same moment, this is but to say that he became no less a man when he became the Chosen Vessel. And for the purposes of the Chosen Vessel it was not loss but gain that he should show the fullest and freest possible play of human feeling. For this does but give the message he conveys a quicker avenue to our human hearts, and assure us that for us, too, the fullest reception of Christ will only develop us into all that is fullest in the nature He has given us.

Chapter xii

THE COLLECTION FOR THE JERUSALEM POOR—
THE FINALE TO ST. PAUL'S WORK IN THE EASTERN
MEDITERRANEAN

2 Corinthians viii. 1-24

WE now find ourselves engaged with Chs. viii and ix of the
Epistle. These deal with the Collection for the poor in Jerusalem,
which figured very largely in St. Paul's mind and plans at this
time. It was indeed the finale of his missionary operations in this
part of the Mediterranean. He was on his third and concluding
missionary journey. He had just spent three years and more of
continuous labour at Ephesus. He was now on the move on a
tour of visitation, bound for Corinth, after which he was to
retrace his steps in a somewhat hurried re-visitation by Macedonia and Asia on the way to Judaea with the money for the poor,
collected and ready to hand over to the officers of the Church
in Jerusalem.

It is with the management of this collection, as we shall see,
that these chapters are concerned. Herein lies their chief significance as lively oracles for the Church, inasmuch as finance is an
essential practical element of church life. But we need to note
that from the beginning of these chapters, and indeed all through
them, as we shall see in the next chapter, the Apostle refers the
whole of this matter of finance to the originating operation of the
grace of God. This he does by opening with the use of the word
χάρις in Ch. viii. 1. But the Greek word appears again and again,
being used in the same chapter no less than seven times, and in
significant positions though with varying turns of meaning. In
v. 1 it stands at the head. In v. 4 it is repeated, showing that it is
not far from the Apostle's mind all the time. 'About the grace
and the participation in the help work designed for the saints',
as we have rendered it. Similarly there are further echoes in
vv. 6 and 7. While in ver. 9, as will be seen, the word introduces

a large doctrinal and dogmatic statement. In ver. 16, where we have translated 'thanks be to God', the same word χάρις in the original introduces the concluding section of the chapter.

The variation of meaning in the use of this beautiful word can be traced from the paraphrase and context. For instance, in ver. 7 it denotes a gift and blessing working in the soul and will, and in ver. 9 it indicates unbought divine kindness in general, while in ver. 16 it may be compared with our grace before meals or thanks to God for His gracious gifts. But all through, even in this ejaculation of thanks to God for giving the same enthusiasm to Titus, there is always present in the writer's mind, as he uses the word, the concept that the church owes its existence to the grace of God, and that the grace of God rests upon it. Thus St. Paul does not regard church finance as a ladder to heavenly things—God forbid! Neither does he take a horizontal view and think of finance merely as a welding force in the life of the church. Rather he looks down into the inner life of the church, and regards all its activities, including its financial arrangements, from the point of view of the grace of God, His gratuitous gift of forgiveness and acceptance, life and health, beauty and glory.

So St. Paul launches out on a fresh topic.[1]

Ver. 1.   **And now we have to inform**[2] **you, brethren, of the grace of our** (τοῦ) **God,** His operative, favouring, presence and power, **which has been given**[3] to hearts and wills, **in the churches,** the mission-congregations, **of Macedonia,** Northern Roman Greece, Philippi, Thessalonica and elsewhere. This grace has come out in the Ver. 2.   fruit of a large and self-denying liberality. **Because under a severe test of trouble,** whether from privation, as in a time of scarcity, or of persecution of the local and social kind,[4] **the overflow of their joy,** their gladness in the Lord, **and,** to give another and paradoxical element in the case, **their utter poverty** (lit. their

---

[1] Hic prorsus alia agitur res (**From here on a fresh matter is put forward**).
[2] γνωρίζομεν—1 Cor. xv. 1; Gal. i. 11.
[3] δεδομένην.
[4] So Acts xi. 19. Cf. Phil. i. 28, 29; 1 Thess. i. 6; ii. 14; iii. 4 (ch. iii is a striking parallel to 2 Cor. vii); 2 Thess. i. 4-6, and see Acts xvi and xvii.

down-to-the-depth poverty), **flowed over to the wealth of their open-handed bounty.**[1]   As it were the two ingredients met; their spiritual joy was great, *and* their poverty was deep[2]; the resultant was

Ver. 3.   the resolve to make all the greater effort to give, and the aggregate was this splendid collection. **Because up to their means, I can assure you, aye, and beyond** ($\pi\alpha\rho\grave{\alpha}$) **their means,** on all ordinary scales of proportionate giving, they came out as **volunteer**[3]

Ver. 4.   benefactors,[4] **with many an appeal begging**[5] **us—about the grace,**[6] this fruit of God's work in them, **and the participation**[7] **in the help-work designed for the saints;** in other words, they pressed it on us as a favour to them to take and convey this grace-prompted collection, through which they took such a noble share in the practical aid designed for the poor Christians at Jerusalem. **Aye, and**

Ver. 5.   the phenomenon did not end there. Their liberality was but the outward manifestation of a previous absolute surrender to the Lord for His work, and to us as His messengers sent to tell them how to do it.   In this sense it was **not** merely **as we expected,** looking (as we did) to see them recognize a Christian duty, and respond in reason to a call upon their means; **no, themselves they gave in the first place to the Lord, and to us,**[8] too, **under the influence of God's will.** Their persons were surrendered, in the deep joy of faith, and therefore and then their purses. 'By means of God's will', drawn and guided by

Ver. 6.   it as the efficient cause, they were at our disposal, ready with their utmost aid.   **The result was that we appealed** (*we* should say, 'are appealing') **to Titus, that he would follow up his** initiation or **inauguration**[9] of your recovery **by proceeding** ($\kappa\alpha\grave{\iota}$) **in the same way to put the last consummate touch** as regards **this grace too,** giving to and collecting from you; in other words we have just been asking Titus now returning with his letter to you, that he should seize the occasion of his visit to stir you up to the exercise of this grace of liberality, the development of which would be the crowning symptom of your renewed spiritual prosperity.

Ver. 7.   **Well then** (the $\grave{\alpha}\lambda\lambda\grave{\alpha}$ of appeal) **just as you are overflowing in everything** in the spiritual life, **faith, and speech, and know-**

---

[1] So ix. 11. Not elsewhere so in New Testament.

[2] Pulcherrimum (**most beautiful**).

[3] So below ver. 17, only here in New Testament.

[4] felices Philippi et Thessalonica! (**Well done, Philippi and Thessalonica!**)

[5] de constructione vid. vs. 24 (**in regard to the construction see ver 24**).

[6] Omit $\delta\acute{\epsilon}\xi\alpha\sigma\theta\alpha\iota$ $\acute{\eta}\mu\tilde{\alpha}\varsigma$.

[7] Grimm explains $\kappa o\iota\nu\omega\nu\acute{\iota}\alpha$ as practically equivalent to collection; and so ix. 13. But we are doubtful.

[8] Sc. ut ipsi nuntii ad Jerusalem irent (?) (**Sc. so that they might go themselves as messengers to Jerusalem (?)**).

[9] $\pi\rho o\epsilon\nu\acute{\alpha}\rho\chi\epsilon\sigma\theta\alpha\iota$ and $\dot{\epsilon}\pi\iota\tau\epsilon\lambda\epsilon\tilde{\iota}\nu$ are both hieratic, cf. Phil. i. 6, and cf. ver. 10, 11 below. $\dot{\epsilon}\pi\iota\tau\epsilon\lambda\epsilon\tilde{\iota}\nu$ can even $=\theta\acute{\upsilon}\epsilon\iota\nu$.

ledge, so that you are conspicuous examples of world-conquering trust, eloquent testimony, and spiritual insight into Christian principle, **and** beside all this **in all** possible **earnestness** for the right, yes, **and,** to come nearer to our own hearts, **in the love** which flows **from you** to lodge itself **in us,**[1] **do see that you overflow**[2] **in this grace too,** the grace of giving. Do not mistake me; this is not said in the imperative

Ver. 8. mood; **I am not speaking in the style of a** *mot d'ordre,* **but** as wishing **to test**[3] **the genuineness of your love** to us, and to the brethren, **using the earnestness of other** Christians as a touchstone. I need not dilate upon the theme, or explain elaborately to you how it lies at the very heart of Christian love to show itself by practical sacrifice;

Ver. 9. **for you know,** without my re-telling, **the grace of our Lord Jesus Christ**—I have been speaking of the grace of sacrifice to be exercised by *you*; think how it was exercised by *Him*; His infinitely gracious action in saving us[4]—you know **that on your account,** for you men and your salvation, **He became poor** (aor.) (we might almost dare to say 'beggared Himself': cf. Phil. ii. 7, ἑαυτὸν ἐκένωσε) **being as He was rich,** on purpose **that you by His poverty might become rich**[5] (aor.). Yes, He was antecedently and eternally wealthy, with the bliss of equality with God, rejoicing always with the Father; when, lo, He stooped to take the creature nature, and its obligations and its limits; to *do without* the use of His divine wealth in those wonderful days of His flesh; so that by His union with us, and in it by His sacrifice for us, He might lift us from the abject poverty of spiritual death to the wealth of those who possess *Him,* as their peace, their purity, their power, their heaven; and possessing Him can say 'all things are ours' (1 Cor. iii. 22).

Here we have ventured on an extended paraphrase and introduced freely dogmatic elements into it. We have a right to do so with the general parallel of Philippians ii before us, written but a few years later, and so obviously on the same general lines of thought. Here as there St. Paul has evidently in view the pre-existence, and consequent sublime free-will of our blessed Lord in His humiliation. He was πλούσιος and became πτωχός, words which have no meaning if they are not referred to a pre-natal state and act. For obviously as incarnate Man He never was

---

[1] pulchrum (**beautiful**).
[2] Cf. ἵνα φοβῆται τὸν ἄνδρα, Eph. v. 33; ἵνα ἐπιθῇς τὰς χεῖρας, Mark v. 23.
[3] non ut exploret amorem sed quia exploratum habet (**not that he may find out the ground of their love but because he has found it**).
[4] 1 John iv, 19.
[5] nos ergo divites in illo (**we therefore are rich in him**). 1 Cor. i. 5.

πλούσιος for a single hour. To quit the earnings of the shop at Nazareth for the life of a teacher dependent upon alms was indeed a touching item in His course of ever deepening self-sacrifice in life (we put on a pedestal sacredly by itself the altar-sacrifice of His death). But that step from πενία (πένης 2 Cor. ix. 9) to πτωχεία, was a very different thing from one from πλοῦτος to πτωχεία. Nothing can naturally explain this language of the Apostle, but the doctrine of the Incarnation; the supreme self-surrender of the Son, 'I come to do Thy will, O my God'.

This being so we may in the first place note the significant passingness of the allusion. It is treated with but a touch. The Apostle only points to it and goes on. And this means that from the very beginning he had taught them the great mystery of salvation. It was no development of a second generation of Christianity. You cannot go so far up into the Origines as ever to find a moment when it was a discovery to the Church, till you come right up to the Christ of the Gospels Himself, and hear Him saying, 'No man knoweth the Son but the Father' (Matt. xi. 27); 'I came forth (Mark i. 38) to preach'; 'I proceeded forth and came from God' (John xvi. 27f.); 'I had glory beside Thee before the world was' (John xvii. 5).

Further let us note here also the profound nexus in apostolic teaching between doctrine and practice. As in Philippians ii so here we have the infinite wonder of the Holy Incarnation. But how, and why? Is it presented as a thing suspended in the air, an isolated and abstract theme of wonder? No; it walks the ground. In Philippians it is given to open the hearts of Christians in unselfish and unenvious sympathy to one another. Here it is given to open the purses of Christians to make a real money-sacrifice for others' good.

Lastly, let us take a positive message from this golden flash of dogmatic light in this most practical passage. It is the divine intention that we, the people of Christ, should be rich, in view of our Redeemer's mysterious poverty. We are to live and act spiritually as those who possess a wealth of life and power in Him. We are to draw upon and to spend up to the limit 'the untrackable wealth of Christ' (Ephes. iii. 8), as regards our condition and action, our experience and service.

This interlude of comment in the midst of our paraphrase is inserted here because we have in this place one of the less frequent cases (in this part of the Epistle as compared with the earlier chapters) of doctrinal deliverance. And in it we have a suggestive example of the great principle of the practicality of dogma in the New Testament; I would rather say, of revealed truth. To put it the other way, we may equally well call it the spirituality of New Testament practice, the perpetual reference of common actions to a supernatural motive in the new life.

Our comment concluded, let us return to the translation.

Ver. 10. **And** accordingly, in view of your Christian insight and maturity, **I do** but **give an opinion in this matter,**[1] as against an order (ἐπιταγή); it is not a matter of compulsion, but it *is* a matter of the highest *fitness*; **for this,** this suggested prompt act of liberality **is in your truest interests. You are those who initiated,** as far back as **a year ago, not only the actual doing** (aor.) this work, **but the being willing** for it; yes, as long ago as that there was not only a first act of collection but a splendid zeal about it. **Well, then, now sum it up,**

Ver. 11. **consummate it with the actual doing also;** (it will do you good—συμφέρει—as consistency and thoroughness always do reflect benefit on those who display them); **so that just as there was** the original **alacrity of your willing, similarly** we may have **too the act of consummation** (aor.), in the resultant bounty for which I am pleading now. And I mean no unreasonable demand; I only look for

Ver. 12. it **from your having,** from your actual resources, such as they are. **For once granted the alacrity** of will, **it is acceptable** to God, and to man, in its results, **in proportion to what a man happens to have, not in proportion to what he has not.** So I mean

Ver. 13. no unfair strain on you; **for it is not that others** may **get relief, you** (omit δέ) **trouble; but on a principle of** (ἐξ)

Ver. 14. **equality,** balance; **just at the present time your** overflow **or surplus to go to their deficit, that,** when the occasion comes, **their surplus may come in for your deficit, so that an**

---

[1] See the curious parallel 1 Cor. vii. 25, περὶ δὲ τῶν παρθένων ἐπιταγὴν κτλ; and cf. ibid. 40, κατὰ τὴν ἐμὴν γνώμην.

equality may result; just as it stands written in the narrative of the

Ver. 15.   manna (Exod. xvi. 18), **'The man with the much had no surplus, and the man with the little had no deficit'.**
That incident was a fact of narrative; but it also was a message of permanent truth. The emphasized points in Israel's exodus have all of them lessons for the wilderness journey of the people of God.

At this point St. Paul turns from speaking of the collection to say a few words about his commissioners. Foremost is Titus, mentioned repeatedly through the Epistle and in important connexions in that part through which we are now passing (e.g. vii. 6, 13, 14; viii. 6, 16, 23). Titus stands out unmistakably as a forceful Christian, one on whom St. Paul could confidently and joyfully rely to present his case with effect. And this in notable contrast with Timothy, a softer character who seems to have possessed different gifts of disinterestedness, understanding, and conciliation (cf. Phil. ii. 20-22). In the present case of the Jerusalem collection, together with Titus we have also the brother 'whose praise is in the Gospel' (ver. 18). That is to say one who already had a reputation in the Churches in furthering the cause of evangelization. It has been suggested that this was St. Luke, and Acts xx. 4-6 gives us to understand that he was the Philippian delegate to Jerusalem in the matter of the collection. But we cannot identify with absolute certainty this brother 'whose praise is in the Gospel'. All we know is that he was a conspicuous missionary worker, and also delegated by the churches to be Paul's and his friends' fellow traveller to Jerusalem. Probably, therefore, he was a Macedonian, assuming that the churches are the Macedonian churches. Much the same must be said of the other brother (ver. 22), who is indicated as perhaps more definitely the practical man in affairs. The same adjective is used of him as of Titus—σπουδαῖος, earnest (vv. 17 and 22).[1]

These, then, were the trio—Titus and two brothers of unknown

---

[1] σπουδαῖος here only in St. Paul and New Testament. The noun σπουδή is used by St. Paul only in the present section of this Epistle (2 Cor. vii. 11, 12; viii. 7, 8, 16) and in the practical conclusion to Romans written shortly afterwards (Rom. xii. 8 and 11). Cf. Heb. vi. 11, and for the adverb, σπουδαίως, Phil. ii. 28; 2 Tim. i. 17; Titus iii. 13.

name but fully established Christian character and well known to the churches. Perhaps they were standing round St. Paul as he dictated. Certainly he knew they were fully prepared to act on his behalf concerning the collection. He knew full well the effect of divine grace in their hearts, and about them and their commission he now writes.

To speak again of Titus. I mentioned just above my appeal to him; and turned aside to appeal to you to meet him in the spirit of full Christian bounty, according to your means. How did Titus meet the suggestion
Ver. 16. made to him? **Now thanks be to our God, who was giving the same enthusiasm regarding you,** an enthusiasm identical in kind with mine, for your interests in respect of your evidencing, by liberality, full Christian consistency, giving this, I say, as a power **in the heart of Titus;** (yes, thanks be to *God;* for all the virtues of His
Ver. 17. saints are ultimately of this gift in grace.) **For as a fact** ($\delta\tau\iota$) **he did, to be sure** ($\mu\grave{\epsilon}\nu$), **accept** and respond to that **appeal;**[1] but that was not all; he was more than ready of his own accord; **finding himself** ($\dot{\upsilon}\pi\acute{\alpha}\rho\chi\omega\nu$) **quite enthusiastic**[2,3] **he is going out** (aor. narrantis)
Ver. 18. **as a volunteer** envoy **to you,** to gather up your loving gifts. **And we are sending along with him** (aor. narrantis) **our brother,** needless to name, **whose praise in the Gospel,**[4] his reputation for zeal and power in evangelization **pervades all the churches,** and
Ver. 19. must therefore be known to you. **And** he goes **not only as thus** *my* selection, recommended to *my* judgement by his high character; not only so, **but as elected**[5] **by the churches,** by the mission-congregations in Macedonia, **as our associate on the journey hence**[6] ($\dot{\epsilon}\kappa$) to Jerusalem, when the time for it comes, **in the matter of this grace,**[7] this bounty, the fruit of the grace of God; this fund **which**

---

[1] Apostoli (**The Apostle's appeal**).

[2] avec un nouveau zêle (**with a fresh zeal**) (Segond): but is this quite true to $\dot{\upsilon}\pi\acute{\alpha}\rho\chi\omega\nu$?

[3] $\sigma\pi\sigma\upsilon\delta\alpha\iota\acute{\sigma}\tau\epsilon\rho\sigma\varsigma$: for such a use of the comparative cf. John xiii. 27; Acts xxv. 10; 2 Tim. i. 18 and Acts xvii. 22, 'very reverent of the supernatural powers'.

[4] For $\epsilon\dot{\upsilon}\alpha\gamma\gamma\acute{\epsilon}\lambda\iota\sigma\nu$ so used cf. Phil. i. 5, 16; iv. 3, 15; 1 Thess. iii. 2.

[5] $\chi\epsilon\iota\rho\sigma\tau\sigma\nu\acute{\epsilon}\omega$: elected by show of hands. The 'show of hands' sinks in usage into the background, e.g. Acts xiv. 23. In Church Greek it is often thus, and Chrysostom uses it of the Lord's choice of labourers for the harvest. It is frequently distinguished from ordination, but *impropriè* comes to equal ordination by imposition of hands.

[6] He *may* therefore have been Sopater of Berea, or Aristarchus, or Secundus of Thessalonica (Acts xx. 4) or Epaphroditus of Philippi.

[7] $\chi\acute{\alpha}\rho\iota\tau\iota$: Sc. in ferendo dono caritatis ecclesiarum (**Sc. in the taking of the gift of the gracious affection of the churches**).

is being administered by us, managed by us, in its collection and its
distribution, to the glory of the Lord (omit αὐτοῦ), to evidence the
blessed power of His love in drawing out heart to heart, and to evidence
our (ἡμῶν) alacrity, to evidence at the same time our cordial eagerness
to help the Church of Jerusalem, missionaries to the Gentiles though
we are.   And this careful association of other agents with us is for a
definite purpose; we do it[1] in order to avoid,[2] to keep clear of,
the risk that anyone might blame us, might find occasion
to criticize us in point of strictest honour and probity, in respect of this
fullness,[3] this rich abundance of donation, which is being (for may I
not take it for granted that so it is in prospect, and will soon
be in act?) supplied by you.   For we take precautions (read
προνοοῦμεν γάρ) for all that is honourable not only before the Lord,
but before men too;[4] we know that it is not enough in this service, to
be right in our own consciences, but to be right in all reasonable human
opinion as well.   And we are sending along with them—
with him and Titus—our brother, yet another friend in
Christ, needless to name, whom we have (aor.) tested many a time
in many a thing and found to be a man of holy enthusiasm, only
now he is far more so than even commonly, with the strong confidence he feels towards you.

Ver. 20.

Ver. 21.

Ver. 22.

Ver. 23.   About Titus?   My partner, in thought and labour, and towards yourselves my fellow worker.   Our brothers
(the two just referred to?) Apostles,[5] holy envoys of the churches,[6]
glory of Christ; men who bear all the prestige of delegation to sacred
work by sacred communities, the mission stations here, and whose
lives reflect to others their Lord's light, winning Him glory.
Such are your present visitors.   I bespeak for them a correspond-
ing welcome then; you will, I know, be giving (read participle) the demonstration of your love to the Lord, and His
poor, and us, and of the verity of our exultation over you, of our
delighted account of what you really are, to them on their arriving,
in face (omit καί) in full view, of the churches, whose eyes will be upon
you, and whose faith will be cheered and strengthened by the sight of
your unity and good will.

Ver. 24.

---

[1] Observe the characteristic freedom of use of the participle.   See above on
vii. 5, θλιβόμενοι.

[2] στέλλεσθαι either simply 'to arrange for oneself', or 'to furl (a sail)', or 'tuck
up (a robe)': so 'avoid', 'keep clear'.

[3] ἁδρότης of a hero's strength in Homer.   Here ἅπαξ λεγ, obviously by context
'richness'.   plenitudo (fullness).   Vulg.

[4] sancta sapientia (holy wisdom).

[5] Phil. ii. 25.

[6] Achaiae et Macedoniae (of Achaia and of Macedonia).

Thus ends our paraphrase of one of the longest chapters in the Epistle, and from certain points of view one of the most remarkable. Here we need only indicate briefly three of its outstanding features; the difficulty of the grammar, the warmth of the sentiment, and the conspicuous wisdom which it displays.[1]

The difficulty of the grammar and therefore of the translation can be seen in the quite unusual degree of italicizing required, for instance, in the Revised Version. We have tried to shed some light on these difficulties in our translation and paraphrase, as far as possible. But they arise in large part from the subject matter which is closely practical and the details of which were far clearer to the writer and his readers than they are to us.

But they arise also out of the combined intensity and delicacy of feeling on the writer's part in regard to these financial matters. With every beautiful artifice of the tact which ultimately means love he engages their interest, their enthusiasm for the matter in hand. Incidentally, he assures them—perhaps with a side glance at the malicious suggestions which no doubt his opponents were ready to make that he was not to be trusted with money—that the greatest care is being taken to give the guarantee of a regular body of trustees when the collection should be complete. No doubt the allusion in ver. 19 to the χειροτονία of the Macedonian churches in the case of the first ἀδελφός, his official assignation to this service, points the same way.

St. Paul with sanctified wisdom wishes to preclude the possibility, where money was concerned, of anyone saying that it was a mere 'one-man arrangement'; as if Paul and a few personal intimates were to have private charge of the whole sum, which would no doubt be a very large one.

---

[1] capitulum 8, grammatice difficile, corde calidum, prudentia insigne (**chapter 8, troublesome in grammar, fervent in sentiment, outstanding in discretion**).

Chapter xiii

THE COLLECTION FOR THE JERUSALEM POOR
—THE LORD'S BOUNTY

2 Corinthians ix. 1-15

As we have already said, Chs. viii and ix form a single and complete section of the Epistle, dealing with the general subject of the Jerusalem collection. At Ch. viii. 16 St. Paul turned aside from the collection to the commissioners. Now, Ch. ix. 1, he turns back again from the commissioners to the collection, with the object of bringing this matter to a close.

Thus much I have written about the general object, the projected collection, and about the enthusiasm for it here, and about Titus and our other friends, and about my assurance that you will on this occasion
Ver. 1. amply evidence the true spirit. In a sense I need not deal in detail with the matter. **For indeed**[1] **about this aid** (διακονία) **intended for the saints,** the Jerusalem Christians, **I feel it** (μοί) **superflous to write to you,** explaining its nature, and setting out its reasons.
Ver. 2. Your interest in it is already engaged. **For I know your alacrity** in the matter; **of that** alacrity, when **on the subject of you, I speak with pride to the Macedonians,** our friends in Christ around me here, saying (ὅτι), **Achaia has been prepared** to come forward **a whole year ago; and your** (not ἐξ ὑμῶν) **zeal,** thus reported, **is what has stimulated the majority of them** (τοὺς πλείονας).[2]

So I think we may explain the otherwise difficult τοὺς πλείονας. The Revised Version has 'very many of them', margin 'the more part'. Segond has, *le plus grand nombre*. Surely we should render οἱ πλείονες by 'the majority' unless the context is very strong against it, as perhaps iv. 15 above? But then, if St. Paul merely means that under the stimulus of his words about Corinth a

---

[1] μὲν γὰρ : μὲν answers to δὲ verse 3.
[2] non omnes (**not all**).

majority of the Macedonians had been roused to generous giving, but only a majority, it would be curiously unlike his exuberant tone about them in the beginning of Ch. viii. Let him be supposed to mean, however, that while all were stirred by *some* means, *most* were stirred by this means—the example of Corinth; this sentence will be quite in harmony with Ch. viii.

To proceed with the paraphrase.

Ver. 3. So you were the first in the field, and I have the less need to write now. **Still** (δέ), there was need—after my high praise of you here to take care that your gifts were promptly ready, to give tangible proof here that I was right about you. So **I am sending** (aor. *narrantis*) **the brethren** of whom I have just spoken **to preclude the possibility of our exultant language,** the language used **over you being stultified in this respect,** however it might prove true in others; **to secure your being, in the words I was using** to the Macedonians, **prepared** with your gifts, and not merely in a general sense interested,

Ver. 4. or willing to give; **for fear that if** any (not 'they of Macedonia' which would be οἱ Μακεδόνες) **Macedonians should accompany me** when I come to you, as I hope soon to do, **and should find you unprepared, we (not to say you) should be put to the blush,** for rose-colour and exaggeration, **in respect of this confidence**[1] (cf. xi. 17; omit τῆς καυχήσεως here) of assertion about your generosity.

Ver. 5. So I have felt it a duty[2] to appeal to these brethren to go on in advance to you, and to make up beforehand[3] **this** already promised (προεπηγγελμένην) **largess**[4] of yours, to be prepared for transmission by us, **thus,** so contributed, not at the last moment but fully in time, **as a largess indeed,** a true 'gift of blessing', accompanied with the giver's warm good will, **and not as if it were a confiscation,** an unfair because forcible levy on your means (*un acte d'avarice*: Segond).

---

[1] Ὑπόστασις: sub-stantia (**the underlying or fundamental essence, substance**); hence what has firmness, and so steadiness, courage, assurance. 'ὑπόστασις in the sense of 'being' or 'nature' is rare: Heb. i. 3 and cf. Wisdom xvi. 21 (R.V.M.). Just possibly some kind of verbal guarantee is indicated by the word here.

[2] Same phrase Phil. ii. 25.

[3] καταρτίζω: to make odd even, or imperfect perfect. So to complete. So to equip.

[4] So Jacob to Esau, Gen. xxxiii. 11; so Caleb to Othniel, Judges i. 15; so Abigail, 1 Sam. xxv 27.

In the verses which we have just paraphrased St. Paul completes what he wishes to say about the practical arrangements in connexion with the collection—the actual gathering in of all the different contributions, the drawing in of the net. The way is therefore clear for him to dwell in conclusion on some of the underlying principles of Christian giving. These, as we have already seen, all spring from the grace of God in the person of Jesus Christ. So he instinctively feels his way again towards the use of the beautiful word χάρις. Seven times the word appeared in the earlier part of what he had to say about the collection, in Ch. viii. Now in this concluding paragraph of Ch. ix he uses the word yet another three times; each time, as before, with fresh significance. Ver. 8: 'Our God is able to make all grace overflow to you'. Here, arising out of the practical issue of sacrificial giving, he has in mind a completely comprehensive view of the supply of divine grace to needy hearts. We shall enlarge a little on that in the midst of our paraphrase further on. Ver. 14: 'the surpassing grace of our God resting upon you'. Here, at the end, we can see him charitably recognizing and rejoicing in the divine grace experienced within. Ver. 15: 'Thanks (χάρις) to our God'. Here is the final note of the passage concerning the practical matter of the collection which has been extended through two whole chapters. Here is the grace which comes from the person of Jesus Christ, returning to God again from truly thankful hearts, rejoicing 'over His indescribable gift'.

So St. Paul, having spoken of their contributions, now goes on to impress upon them the resultant blessings, which he is at pains to show will be according to the spirit in which they have contributed.

Ver. 6.   **Now take note here**[1]**—the man who sows sparingly, sparingly too shall reap, and the man who sows on terms of largess,**[2] **on terms of largess too shall reap; the full**

---

[1] Perhaps supply λέγω: so Vulgate and R.V. But is it not enough to take it as, 'here is *this*'—'look *here*'? No parallel appears in St. Paul.

[2] lit. 'on blessings'—with εὐλογίαι as his conditioning scale. So ἐπὶ τῇ πίστει, Phil. iii. 9.

Ver. 7. willing gift shall be met by the like from the Lord. **Each just as he has** (perfect) **purposed in his heart,** not on a mechanical scale; it must be absolutely voluntary, as between the man and his Lord; **it must not be** ($\mu\grave{\eta}$) **under pain or under pressure** (lit., 'out of'; resulting from the pain of reproach, or pressure, necessity, of mere *comme-il-faut*); **for a glad giver our** ($\acute{o}$) **God loves.   But**
Ver. 8.   there is another side, too; the God who asks is also the God who gives; **our God is able to make all grace overflow to you,** so to act to you in His free favour that its gifts, of what sort, as there is need, shall be more than equal to the demand, **so that having in all things always all sufficiency you,** in your turn, **may flow over,** passing on your blessings in loving beneficence, **to all good works.**[1]

Here is a golden verse to be weighed and used.   To be *weighed* in a daily reaffirmation and recollection of our faith in the person of the great Lord of all grace.   See how heavily freighted is this verse with every possible gift of grace—'all grace', 'in all things', 'all sufficiency', 'to all good works'.   The verse is also to be *used* to claim daily, in the name of the same Lord, the supply of grace we need, wherever we may be and whatever may be the outward circumstances in which we find ourselves placed.   The Greek word for sufficiency is $\alpha\dot{v}\tau\acute{\alpha}\rho\kappa\epsilon\iota\alpha$—literally 'such a supply on the spot as to be independent of externals'.

So, then, let the Christian daily renew his vows in the Lord of all grace in all things, for all sufficiency, unto all good works.

And let him make it a personal *Credo—I* believe.

> I believe in the Name of The Son of God.
> Therefore I am in Him, having redemption through His blood, and life by His Spirit.
> And He is in me, and all fullness is in Him.
> To Him I belong, by purchase, conquest and self-surrender.
> To me He belongs, for all my hourly need.
> There is no cloud between my Lord and me.
> There is no difficulty, inward or outward,
> which He is not prepared to meet in me today.
> The Lord is my Keeper.—AMEN.

---

[1] For the Bishop's note in the margin of his Greek Testament against ver. 8, see Appendix A last paragraph but one, and footnote 2, p. 134.

Our comment here is a devotional note, as it were in the margin of the text.

Returning, therefore, to the text itself, and to our translation, we see that St. Paul confirms what he says by a quotation, and then proceeds to the end of the chapter.

Ver. 9.   **Just as it stands written** (Ps. cxii. (cxi.) 9: verb) in words which describe such fullness and freedom of holy giving, **'He scattered, he gave to the poor** (πένησιν); **his righteousness abides for ever:'** his Master says over him, with an eternal meaning in it, 'Well done, good and faithful'. So may it be with you to whom I write.

Ver. 10.   **Now He who furnishes seed to the sower** in our fields, year by year, **and so bread for food**—giving to the sower that so the sower may provide for the consumer—**He will** (read future) **furnish and will multiply your seed,** will give you means for these sacred bounties, **and so will increase the products,** the 'yield' **of your righteousness,** the harvest of your joy hereafter when He shall say with the greater joy, '*Well done, good and faithful*'. So I return to the assurance that God is able to supply you that you may ever be able to

Ver. 11.   give in His service—**in all things kept enriched** (pres. part.) **for all,** for full, liberality, such as (ἥτις) **works out, by means of us** (us, your agents and intermediaries to convey gift to

Ver. 12.   recipient) **thanksgiving to our God. Because the test of this service,** the help conveyed through our action as trustees of your alms, **is not only in the way to fill up[1] the** monetary deficiencies of the Jerusalem **Christians, but also to overflow,** to do much more than its direct good, quickening and warming hearts, **by means of many thanksgivings to God;** it will make many a Christian happier and holier by filling him with gratitude for the existence of such

Ver. 13.   living Christians at Corinth. Yes, **they will be** (free participial construction) **under the influence of** (διὰ c. gen.) **the** satisfactory **test of this aid,** the evidence of your genuine fellowship given in your alms, **glorifying our** (τὸν) **God, on occasion of the subjection,[2]** the loyalty of spirit and action, **prompted by your confession in view of the Gospel of our** (τοῦ) **Christ,** your glad recognition of all its blessings as you look on it in its reality; **and by the liber-**

---

[1] Cp. xi. 9. προσαναπληρόω.
[2] Sc. obedientia per quam declaraverant amorem evangelii et discipulorum ejus (Sc. the obedience through which they had declared their love of the gospel and of its disciples).

ality of your impartation of your means for them and for all;
Ver. 14. yes, and they will glorify Him, too, on occasion of their
own petition for you, as they feel their hearts all the happier
while they call down blessings on such loving givers, yearning for you,
feeling they would give anything to see you, because of the surpassing
grace of our (τοῦ) God resting upon you. Wonderful grace! What
can it not do, in us, through us, in results of boundless blessings? It is
all of Him!

Ver. 15. Thanks (we cannot give the play, as French can: grâces soient
rendues—Segond) to our (τῷ) God over His indescribable
gift![1] (super inenarrabili dono ejus. Vulg.).

Thus St. Paul brings to a close this section of his Epistle,
extended through Chs. viii and ix and dealing with the subject of
the collection for the poor in Jerusalem. The thought of Divine
grace has never been far absent from his mind. He used the word
frequently at the beginning of Ch. viii. He returns to it again
with added emphasis as this chapter draws to its close.

'Thanks be to God for His indescribable gift'. The words are
at once a challenge and a charge. A challenge never to forget that
'God so loved the world that He gave His only-begotten Son,
that whosoever believeth in Him should not perish but have
everlasting life'. A charge to give as He gave. Thus he stands at
the end with his finger pointing to the sky—'Thanks be to God
for His indescribable gift'.

---

[1] John iii. 16; or is he referring to superabundant grace?

Chapter xiv

ST. PAUL'S APOLOGIA—ALONGSIDE HIS RIVALS

2 Corinthians x. 1-18

WE now approach the closing portion of the epistle. The Apostle
has uttered his heart to the Corinthians on a variety of subjects.
In Ch. i-vi inclusive he has dealt with many matters of spiritual
truth and spiritual life, in close connexion with circumstances
indeed, but with a main view to their edification. Then he has
passed, in Ch. vii, to his personal relations with Corinth, and the
peculiar happiness which Titus' report upon their general state
of mind had given him; all with a view to bringing their hearts
into closer contact with his own by evidencing his intense affection
for them, and the all-importance of Corinth to his personal
happiness. Then in Chs. viii and ix we have seen him turning
direct to the question of the Jerusalem Fund, so much upon his
heart.

But now another subject presses itself upon him. He must
speak in closing of the teachers at Corinth who were his determined and unscrupulous opponents, and who still had too much
attention given them. He must expose them, and in some sort
he must deliberately, and with a sense of duty, assert himself, as
the messenger of Christ. What precisely led him to reserve this
to the close of the epistle, instead of dealing with it earlier, we
cannot possibly know for certain. We have no reason to think
that St. Paul elaborately planned his epistles, mapping out the
subjects in a table of contents. In a mind of such vivacity as his
this was unlikely. And the guidance of The Holy Ghost would
in no respect, that we can see, be likely to modify the perfectly
free progress of his thought, in which subject after subject arose
in an order suggested perhaps by very minute accidents. How
possible that these last chapters should hardly have been in his
view at all when he began! And then how possible that as the

letter grew, and no doubt the work was interspersed with conversation, he should have become acutely conscious that, with all that was cheering at Corinth, this danger from thoroughgoing opponents was still present there, and might spoil everything! And then he would address himself to meet it, in gravest earnest.

However, here we have this 'Four Chapter Section'. It contains precious gems of divine message, in words now for ever dear to the church. But its main substance is stern and energetic reproof.

Let us take up the words as they stand.

Ver. 1.   **But**[1] now to turn to another and grave matter; **I, personally, Paul,** as directly as possible, have to make an **appeal to you, using as my argument the meekness and the unselfish kindliness** (equity, the equity which can see the other's point of view, cf. Phil. iv. 5 —'meekness in action') **of our Christ,** reminding you of the spirit which He exemplified, and which He inspires, and trusting you to act accordingly. *I* make this appeal, the man **who am,** as the opinion goes, when meeting you **face to face, down in the dust**[2] **among you,** hardly daring to hold my own in thought or action, but when away, when safe **at a distance, am all courage towards you.** Such is the picture of me so often drawn. Believe me, it is so far true that I long to have no occasion to be anything but meek and mild at Corinth; it is just my fear that I may be obliged, to my own great pain, to be 'full of courage' in person there against certain persons. **But,** as I say, **I do make a petition,** a petition that you would be resolute for the old Gospel and not parley with the new, **so that I may not, when present,** when again face to face with you, **come out** (aor.) **in the courage** of sternest action **with that resolution with which I reckon,** from appearances, that **I must make** (aor.) **a front attack upon certain people,** those I mean **who reckon us as men who walk flesh-wise,**[3] who guide conduct and action by unspiritual principles, and so trim our sails to the winds of opportunism. **True, we walk,** we live and behave, **in flesh,**[4] under the inevitable limitations of human weakness, so as, for example, to be compelled to change a plan which had seemed the best to our imperfect view. **But not flesh-wise**[5] **do we carry on**

Ver. 2.

Ver. 3.

---

[1] Aliam hic rem tractat (**At this point he deals with another subject**).
[2] Ver. 10.
[3] morali sensu (**in a moral sense**).
[4] spirituali sensu (**in a spiritual sense**).
[5] corporali sensu (**in a physical sense**). Gal. ii. 20.

our spiritual campaign; in the sense of 'flesh' which means man's will and wisdom apart from God. That campaign is, in essence, the delivery of the Gospel; and there, because *it* is heavenly and eternal, we are as immoveable as the commission of our Master can make us. **(For the weapons of our warfare are not fleshly,** the arms and armour of mere human thought and scheme, **but powerful** by relation **to**[1] **our God,** because conditioned by Him as their Maker and Giver, **with a view to the demolition of fortifications,** the bulwarks of prejudice, and pride, and custom, and the deceitfulness of sin.) Yes, so we carry on our campaign (observe the continuity of con-struction with ver. 3). And so we deal with the castles of the foe, **demolishing** not stone walls but **reasonings,** the argu-mentations of the unconverted heart against its need of Christ, and against His glory and His claims, **and every elevation,** as it were the towers and keeps of the world of sin, which is **reared to dominate the knowledge of our God;** the whole attitude which looks down upon a message which preaches a God not of metaphysics, nor of idolatry, but of man-humbling salvation; **and** then **taking** the garrison as well as levelling the fort—making **prisoner** of **every thought,** every anti-Christian suggestion of the soul, to reduce it **to the obedience of,** due to be demanded by, **our Christ; and,** when the work of conquest is happily done, in unconverted hearts, then—unwillingly but in duty—to chastise obstinate rebels; **holding things in readiness to take vengeance for**[2] **all disobedience,**[3] **when once your obedience shall be completed.**[4]

Ver. 4.

Ver. 5.

Ver. 6.

In these verses St. Paul encourages those who supported him, and differentiates them from those who tried to make him suspect, charged him with insincerity, and accused him of mercenary motives, of lack of apostolic authority, and of not preaching the Gospel. This differentiation he effects by a vigorous appeal to the spiritual warfare in the cause of the Gospel (ver. 3f.) and by a declaration (ver. 6) that those who wilfully hinder the work may at the end of the campaign find themselves excluded. This is what he means by 'holding things in readiness to take vengeance for all dis-obedience, when once your obedience shall be completed'. In other words his campaign, when it brings him and his com-panions to Corinth, will find them true to their work as the Lord's

---

[1] 'before' (R.V.) cf. Acts vii. 20.
[2] Not 'on': cf. Rev. vi. 10.
[3] παρακοήν Sc. aliorum non ὑμῶν (**Sc. of others not of yours**).
[4] Pulchra pericope tropica (**a fine figurative passage**). Vs. 3-6.

forces. His first care will be, indeed (he cannot help saying this, by the way), to aid all loyal hearts to understand God's truth, that they may fully do His work. But then, should opponents to his Gospel still resist, it will be his duty to meet them with the sternness of reproof and with the judicial rod of solemn banishment from the church.

Having written thus, he now writes more pointedly concerning those who were casting reflections on his authority.

Ver. 7. **Take care**[1] **about the things**[2] which will have to be done when we are **face to face.**[3] It will be a stern question then between claim and claim to immediate connexion with the Lord. **Whoever is sure,** with an assurance resting on himself,[4] **that he is Christ's,**[5] Messiah's man in a distinctive sense, one of the school, perhaps leader of the school, which calls itself οἱ Χριστοῦ, **let him go back** (πάλιν) **and,** amidst his many 'reckonings', **reckon in regard of himself,** as a fact bearing on himself, this, **that exactly as he is Christ's,** Messiah's man, **so too are we** His men (omit Χριστοῦ).

St. Paul means, undoubtedly, we are very much more so. It might be put—'that he, to put it gently, has not one whit more claim to know Christ's nature and message than we'. Probably he refers to the charge that he, Paul, was not an 'original' Apostle: but, then, neither were his rivals. And he, Paul, does claim, as they seemingly did not, a supernatural after-commission.

So, too, I say are we οἱ Χριστοῦ, and we shall have to act as such, and to show that the written forewarning was no mere idle thunder, *brutum*
Ver. 8.   *fulmen.* **For if I should** even **somewhat largely boast of our authority,** our full authoritative apostolate (**which,**

---

[1] βλέπετε: Whether is this interrogative, assertive, or imperative? We incline to the latter.
[2] He takes up probably the κατὰ πρόσωπον of ver. 1. He was charged with keeping 'out of sight'. Well, let them look at the facts about those who were 'in sight'.
[3] 'Take care about the things face to face'. This rendering is tentative.
[4] Cf. Phil. i. 14.
[5] 1 Cor. i. 12.

meanwhile, **the Lord gave** (omit ἡμῖν) **in order to your building up and not to your demolition**[1] – evangelization is its ἔργον, spiritual punishment its sad, unwilling, πάρεργον—**I shall not be shamed** by the facts when I come to put it in exercise. I say this to apprise you that I am not acting on the plan of sending severe letters, never to be followed up;

Ver. 9.   **that I may not seem** as if somehow (ὡς ἂν) I were wishing **to scare you**[2] off what I disapprove **by means of the letters** I write, meaning little or nothing in practice. This, you know, is what

Ver. 10.   my opponents say; **for, his letters, to be sure** (μὲν), **they say** (φησί), **are severe**[3] **and vigorous; but the presence of his person,** his personnel, **is weak,**[4] **and his discourse,** his style, **despicable.**[5]

Ver. 11.   **Such a person** as this critic **must** please to **reckon this** for a fact, **that what we are in** respect of **utterance, by letters while away** from you, **just such** shall we be, **when present** with you, **in respect of action.**

Now follows a sentence of severe irony.

Ver. 12.   There are indeed *some* points about which we are timid. **We do not dare**[6]—it would be presumptuous no doubt—**to class ourselves amongst, or to compare ourselves with, certain** specimens **of** the race of **self-recommenders;** a foolish race; **aye** (ἀλλὰ), **themselves measuring themselves among themselves,**[7] **and comparing themselves with themselves**—in fact, a school of mutual admiration—well, I will not say anything more than that—**they do not**

Ver. 13.   **understand** things as they are; they live in a paradise of fools. **As for us** we have indeed our boasts and claims, and, among them, the claim to be your lawful spiritual guides, as being your original

---

[1] Sc. re et actione probabitur auctoritas nostra (**Sc. authority will be really demonstrated by execution**).

[2] Deut. xxviii. 26, of frightening off birds.

[3] Or perhaps grave, weighty—βαρύτερα τοῦ νόμου, Matt. xxiii. 23. But cf. Acts xx. 29. λύκοι βαρεῖς.

[4] Paulus procul dubio aliquid infirmi habebat in habitu corporis et in elocutione (**Paul, it can hardly be doubted, had some weakness of bearing and delivery**). Cf. xi. 6.

[5] Almost 'beneath contempt'. Cf. however Luke xxiii. 11 of Herod's mockery of Our Blessed Lord. Or is it (see ver. 11) 'His written utterances may be laughed at'? Here are words which indicate an element of truth—very suggestively and instructively, cf. ver. 1.

[6] Sc. nos ipsos nimis vere novimus (**Sc. we are too well acquainted with ourselves**).

[7] ἐν ἑαυτοῖς—inter se (**between themselves**).

and apostolic evangelists, within the lines of The Lord's commission. As for us, **our boast shall not go out of our limits;**[1] we have no need to trespass an inch on others' fields when we say, Corinth is ours in Christ! **It will be** (ἀλλά) strictly **according to the limit of the province,** the limit **which our** (ὁ) **God delimited to us—to extend**[2] **as**

Ver. 14. **far as even you.**[3] **Yes, we are not unduly**[4] **stretching ourselves out** in our claim of sphere of influence, **as if we did not really extend up to you;** as if we were assigned to another Christian power; **for actually up to you we were first in the field**[5] **in the missionary enterprise of our Christ.** Thus we are **not carry-**

Ver. 15. **ing our boastings,** our claim of victories, our assertion of spiritual possession, **into regions not delimited to us, in the toils,** in the field of toil, **belonging to others**; no, we confidently claim you as within our bounds, and claim liberty to advance from you into a still unoccupied hinterland in the West; we 'boast' **as having a hope, now your faith is growing** (for such a growth will be a grand assistance to our own faith and enterprise), **to be amongst you,** during our coming visit to you, **reinforced** in point of both spiritual and material equipment and resource (still quite **within our province,** 'according to our line' of allotment), reinforced and aggrandized, I say,

Ver. 16. **to** capacity for **overflow,**[6] for new egression upon heathendom; in other words **for carrying the gospel into the regions beyond you;** regions as yet untouched by any evangelistic effort; **not** as wishing **to assert** claims and victories **within an alien province,** invading a district **ready to hand,** already visited and worked.[7]

Ver. 17 I use the word 'boast' again and again, in these words about assertion and claim; but let me do it in the right spirit, and let others do the like: **'the man who boasts, in the Lord let him boast,'**[8] and in the Lord alone. **For the self-recommender, not he,** I say, **is**

Ver. 18. **the man to take as genuine,** the *probatus vir*, tested and passed, **but he whom the Lord recommends,** he who has the testimonials of the Lord, His verification of His servant by His own sign manual in the servant's word, work, and spirit.

---

[1] Sc. extra opus nobis a Deo datum (**Sc. beyond the work given to us by God**).

[2] certe (**certainly**).

[3] Sc. vos revera nostri gregis estis (**Sc. you in fact are part of our flock**).

[4] Sc. quasi licentiam Domini non habeamus Corinthum evangelizare (**Sc as though we did not have the Lord's licence to evangelise Corinth**).

[5] ἐφθάσαμεν—*primi* advenimus (**we were the first to come**).

[6] sc. Dominus etiam ultra vos jussit nos evangelizare (**The Lord also commanded us to evangelise beyond you**).

[7] id quod antipaulinistae faciebant (**just what the anti-Paulinists were doing**).

[8] 1 Cor. i. 31, cf. Jer. ix. 24.

Many a Christian minister and worker following in the steps of St. Paul has had to meet like difficulties in his ministry and labours. The chapter which we have just completed he may take as his model and guide. He may test his rivals and their claims as St. Paul did along the line of the character of their teaching, the basis of their appointment, the quality of the approval which they receive and welcome, the degree of legalistic argument to which they resort, the premium which they put upon themselves and the infallibility of their own ideas of the will of Christ, all coupled with the extent to which they adopt a superior attitude not merely in words but deeds.

At the same time he will use this chapter as an apostolic model on which to conduct the campaign in the name of Christ against such rivals and their teaching and practices. He will make each spiritual thought of St. Paul a heading of prayer for himself—for the meekness and gentleness of Christ, for firm resolution in prosecution of the Gospel campaign even to the end, for fervency of spirit which enlists loyal hearts by its burning sincerity, for determination to bring every thought into captivity to the obedience of Christ, for fearlessness in meeting others, for assurance in his own calling and gifts, for the strength and grace of Christ in his natural weaknesses, for resolution to prove himself a workman which needeth not to be ashamed in every department of the sphere allotted to him in the Divine Wisdom.

Thus at the end of each day as he works his way, sometimes through painful personal difficulties, this will be his criterion—The Lord's recommendation and not man's—and this will be his prayer:

> From all this day has brought me, I come apart to Thee,
>> O dear and Sovereign Master.
> For all that Thou hast been to me each hour,
>> I bless Thee.
> For everything which of Thy mercy Thou hast done through me,
>> I give Thee humble thanks.
> All transgression and short coming,
> even in the most secret thought,
>> I now confess and renounce.

I lay it on Thy head for pardon,
and under Thy feet for deliverance.
Thou dost accept and deliver me even now.
Now more than ever I own myself Thine,
night and day.
Thy bondservice is my one and perfect freedom.
It is good thus to live day by day to Thee,
my LORD, my LIFE,
and to lie down night by night
beneath Thy smile.

AMEN

Chapter xv

ST. PAUL'S APOLOGIA
—HIS APOSTOLIC AUTHORITY

2 Corinthians xi. 1-33

So the Apostle has entered on his painful task, and has boldly placed himself alongside his rivals with the deliberate claim to regard Corinth as his own evangelistic and apostolic province. Over it the Lord, and no less a power, has given him the sacred claim of His commission and of His blessing upon the work. The spiritual campaign at Corinth was opened by Paul and his helpers, and carried by them to victory; rival and discordant evangelism can never assert with truth that great fact for itself. Strong in that conviction, Paul when he visits Corinth will visit it with a consciousness of Christ-given power, to be exercised in stern spiritual discipline if need be. Far from asking for welcome as a favour, he will come as a *legatus* into his own assigned *provincia*, and as purposing to use it as a basis of operations upon a further region, in the name of the *Imperator* of the Church.

As he now proceeds, after a pause, we seem to see him filled with a yet deeper and stronger emotion of love on the one hand, an indignation, even to a certain sanctified scorn upon the other. He bursts into impassioned language about his intense and intimate relations with Corinth; a strange vagary of Corinthian feeling which can now take meekly the harshest treatment from his rivals, while so sensitive to warnings from himself; the utter and manifested disinterestedness of his own dealings with them; the unholy hollowness of his opponents' spirit and intentions; his own overwhelming proofs of apostolical authority, if there is such a thing as a credential given by unmeasured toil and suffering in the work of the Lord who bade him go and preach His word.

Our present chapter begins with some abruptness:

Ver. 1.   **Would**[1] **that you bore with me just a little** (μικρόν τι), bore
with folly supposed to be shown by me. **Well, now, do really**
(καί) **bear with me;** while I speak in the folly of burning love. **For I**
Ver. 2.   **am jealous over** (zealous for) **you, with God's own
jealousy** (zeal), **for I** (not emphatic) **betrothed you,**[2] I, like
Abraham's steward with Rebekah, procured your betrothal **to one
Husband,**[3] never to have a rival; **to present you** (for the betrothal was
instantly followed by the actual spiritual union) **a pure virgin,** in the
warmth of first love, **to our Christ.** This my blessed function seemed
Ver. 3.   to be all successfully discharged. **But now I am afraid lest
somehow,** just **as the Serpent,** in the primal temptation,
cheated Eve, cozened her out the purity and bliss of simple reliant
obedience, **by his unscrupulous craft, so your thoughts should be
corrupted,** spoiled, and diverted **from the simplicity (and the
purity)**[4] **which has regard to our Christ,** and to Him alone.

Paul's feeling in this whole matter is a passion but a hallowed
passion, caught from the heart of God Who cares infinitely for
His people and for their loyalty to His truth. It cannot be otherwise with him. He was the agent of their spiritual betrothal,
and he sees them in peril of being drawn away from their Lord
and Spouse. He is concerned for the blessed attitude which sees
in Him the *sole* way of salvation, the *sole* object of satisfaction and
desire, and the unsullied life of perfect love which results, directed
towards Him. His evidence for this fear is the surprising patience
with which they are listening to the exponent of a totally different
message, aye, a totally different Saviour.

Ver. 4.   **For if,** as is the fact (or is it not?) **the person**[5] **coming**[6] **to
you,** the new arrival since my departure, **is proclaiming**

---

[1] ὄφελον = ὤφελον: lit., 'I ought', e.g. θανεῖν. Then it falls out of construction
and is taken, as here, in appeal to others and with indicatives: e.g. 1 Cor. iv. 8.
[2] Middle.
[3] N.B.—this holy metaphor Romans vii. 4; Eph. v. 25-27.
[4] W.H. text, but with brackets.
[5] Here, perhaps, and in some other places St. Paul seems to allude to a
single, leading representative of the new school; not solitary but prominent.
If so paraphrase 'the person coming to you'—'quisquis is sit de tempore in
tempus' (whoever he may be from time to time).
[6] The present is difficult. Perhaps we may paraphrase the new teacher 'on
his arrival'.

10   105

another Jesus, whom we did not proclaim, a quite different conception of both the Person and the Work of the Man of Nazareth, **or if,** as is the fact, **you are receiving,** as is alleged, in connexion with such teaching, **a different** (ἕτερον) **Spirit, which you did not receive** from us, alleged 'gifts', but issuing in a whole different temper and character, **or** again **a different Gospel, which you did not accept** certainly from us, a message speaking very differently both of the character and the remedy of Sin, **you bear grandly¹ with him!**

Paul realizes that such an exponent enjoys respectful audiences, admiring comments. What clearness of theory, what strictness of religious precepts, how reasonable, how clear, how good! Has he not just reason to fear that the Christ of his first love is no longer followed by a faithful Bride? Paul, moreover, is aware of certain particular aspects of their teaching. How they dinned into the ears of their audiences that the great Original Teachers of Jerusalem were alone the depositories of truth—men beloved and commissioned by the Lord indeed, but put into a totally false position by this emissary who exploits them to support his own errors. Therefore he is bound to speak in strong terms of pain. He is determined to affirm that he himself has indeed full credentials as the Lord's inspired messenger to them.

Ver. 5. **For I reckon that I have in no respect** so far as you have evidence, **fallen short of the superlative apostles,² If I**
Ver. 6. **actually am,³** as they say, just **an ignoramus⁴ in my speech⁵** my utterance, my oral presentation of truth, **still, I am not such in my knowledge,** in my God-given certainty of the truth He has revealed to me; **no,** we are men **who in every respect made** that **clear** (φανερώσαντες)⁶, ⁷ **among all men,** wherever we worked and taught, **towards you,⁸** so as to bring reasonable conviction to your minds.

---

¹ Sc. horum se exaltantium ut apostolos, false (**Sc. of those who are exalting themselves as apostles, falsely**), καλῶς ironice (**ironically**). Cf. Mark vii. 9, fortbien (**well and strong**)—Segond.
² ces apôtres par excellence (**these superlative apostles**).—Segond.
³ omit δὲ in translation.
⁴ A layman, an amateur, a non-professional: cf. Acts iv. 13.
⁵ x. 10.
⁶ ut apostolo (**as an apostle**).
⁷ See iv. 2.
⁸ ver. vi. b. mira brevitas orationis (**wonderful brevity of speech**).

Corinth, as St. Paul and the Corinthians knew very well, was able to gather his credentials to inspiration not only from discourses at Corinth, but from reports from every quarter of the apostle's own wide field. But he knew that there was also another charge. This had to do with his refusal to take their money for himself. This charge he now takes up.

Ver. 7.　**Or did I commit a sin in laying myself low,**[1] as a man obliged to work for his daily bread, and accepting alms from poor people far off, **just in order** (by the way) **that you might be lifted aloft** in Gospel blessings (by having, as I hoped, my message thus commended to you), **I mean because gratis I preached to you the Gospel of our God? Other Churches I plundered,**[2] like a Ver. 8.　raider, accepting their money to pay my way, **taking wages** of them, making myself, as it were, their agent, **with a view to your** better **service,** so as to give you spiritual ministrations which Ver. 9.　evidently were not designed to squeeze money out of you; **aye, when present with you, and at a crisis of money-difficulty**[3] **I did not burthen**[4] with appeals **a single person** among you. **For my deficiency was adequately** ($\pi\rho\delta s$) **supplied**[5] **by my brethren,**[6] I mean on their coming from Macedonia.[7] **And** indeed **in every respect I watchfully kept myself unburthensome to you, and I will do so still.**[8] **Sure as Christ's truth is in me,** lodged Ver. 10.　in my heart, my message, and my all, **this boast shall not be closed against me,** shut like a door in my face, made impossible for me to use, so far as my action can secure it **in the region** Ver. 11.　**of your Achaia. And why? Because I don't love you,** and so dislike to be under obligations to you? **Our God** Ver. 12.　**knows! But what I am doing I will persist in;**[9] this policy of gratuitousness as regards your purses, **on purpose to cut clean** ($\dot{\epsilon}\kappa$-) **away the pretext of these people who want a pretext for being found,** pronounced, **in the matter of their glorying, just where we are**—just as much or as little disinterested as we.

---

[1] 1 Cor. iv. 11, 12, 13.
[2] Phil. iv. 10, 15.
[3] $\dot{\nu}\sigma\tau\epsilon\rho\eta\theta\epsilon\dot{\iota}s$ cf. Phil. iv. 11, 12.
[4] See xii. 13.
[5] $\pi\rho\sigma\sigma\alpha\nu\alpha\pi\lambda\eta\rho\delta\omega$ ix. 12.
[6] Paraphrastic construction for order's sake.
[7] Macedonia paupera Corintho diviti subvenit: (**Macedonia the poor reinforced Corinth the rich**). Acts xviii. 5—when Silas and Timothy came down from Macedonia.
[8] Paraphrase.
[9] Mais j'agis et j'agirai de la sorte (**but I take action and will take action in this way**).—Segond.

St. Paul takes this line in order that his opponents may be unable to have the excuse, in their own demands upon the Corinthians for subsidy and support, of saying that Paul and his friends do just the same. He intends to point out that such manoeuvres on their part are all in character.

Ver. 13. **For persons of this sort are sham-apostles,** false in claim and so, inevitably, in action, **crafty work-people,** advocates of work-salvation[1] **putting on the disguise of Christ's apostles,**[2] professing a special delegation from the genuine Christ, while all the while their 'Christ' is no Christ at all. **And no wonder; for** Ver. 14. **Satan,** the (ὁ) supreme Adversary, **himself puts on the disguise of an angel of light,**[3] being all the while 'the world-ruler of the darkness' (Eph. vi. 12, cf. Acts xxvi. 18).[4] **So it is no great** Ver. 15. **thing if his agents too put on the disguise of agents of righteousness,**[5] claiming to be stern moralists, being all the while opponents of the truth which alone ultimately secures absolute morality —free grace; **whose end will be according to their works,** the end of destruction (Phil. iii. 19), the Master's 'I never knew you', if they persist.

All the while St. Paul knows, and he must reassert it—every credential which his opponents claim is possessed and surpassed by himself. He *has* evidence enough for his apostleship to claim their faith for his message. He must repeat his appeal to them to tolerate his supposed 'folly' in what looks like self-assertion. Folly it is *not*, as a fact. But, even if it be, he wishes them to bear with him, while he expresses what they may take, if they please, as a mere personal statement (vv. 16-17).

---

[1] Cf. perhaps Phil. iii. 2.

[2] These phrases must be noted in considering the meaning of ver. 5. They incline to explanations there of the propagandists as οἱ ὑπερλίαν ἀπόστολοι.

[3] in libro Hiob? **(in the book of Job?).**

[4] To what is the reference? Possibly to our Lord's Temptation, though no detail of the narrative there quite illustrates this. Possibly to his appearing 'with the sons of God' in the opening scene of Job. But also possibly the reference is purely spiritual and moral.

[5] Let us not hastily say, this is harsh and uncharitable. The propagandist of an anti-Gospel is, whether he knows it or not, an agent of the Adversary of Christ. See Acts xiii. 10 υἱὲ διαβόλου.

Ver. 16.   **I go back** (πάλιν) on previous words (ver. 1), and **I say, do not let anyone think me foolish,** for this iteration of my claims; I do not so without facts, and not without urgent reason; it is not to advertise myself but to insist on the claims of my Master's message. **But if you quite refuse,**[1] **still receive me,** to tolerate me, **even if** (you receive me) **as a foolish person;** that is, with the half-contemptuous patience you would accord to a weak-witted but harmless being;

Ver. 17.   **that I too,** as well as my rivals, **may glory just a little. What I speak,** this coming utterance about myself, **not at the Lord's instance do I speak,** not as directly prompted or authorized by Him[2] (cf. 1 Cor. vii. 6 (by permission), 12) **but as in foolishness,**[3] claiming no more for it, in the first instance, than the attention you would give to a harmless being not quite sane; as in foolishness I say, **in this con-**

Ver. 18.   **fidence**[4] **of my** (τῆς) **glorying,** this tone of assurance in trumpeting my claims.   **Since many persons,** these numerous rivals of mine, **are glorying—flesh-wise,** on principles which are not those of the grace of God, **I too**—I do not say, will glory flesh-wise, self-fully and for self—but **will glory,** will assert my position. And may I not expect your benevolent attention? For you are very willing

Ver. 19.   to give it in other and apparently similar cases. **(For you are sweetly tolerant of the foolish, being** yourselves so **sapient;** moved by your own deep wisdom (may I speak with gentle irony?) to be

Ver. 20.   so. **For you tolerate,** you put up even meekly, from what I hear of your attitude towards these emissaries, **with people when they**[5] **make slaves of you** in spiritual despotism, **when they eat you up** with extortion, **when they take** your property, **when they are arrogant** in tone, **when they give you slaps in the face**—by contemptuous words about your position as mere outsiders, till you

Ver. 21.   have humbly sought admission to the Jewish circle of privilege). **I speak in terms of dishonour,** of disgrace;[6] of conduct which assumes our claims and our privileges to be despicable; **as if we have proved weak,** have turned out to be helpless to maintain our

---

[1] *Μήγε: γε* underlining *μή.* Supply *εἰ δὲ μήγε θέλετε οὕτω ποιεῖυ.*

[2] Note (i) the tacit witness of such a phrase to his normal consciousness (or certainty) of inspired guidance. 'Theopneusta sunt igitur, et secundum Dominum dicta, quaecunque Paulus sine hac expressa exceptione scripsit. . . .' (Therefore whatever Paul wrote, with this express exception, is God-breathed and spoken after the Lord).—Bengel, q.v.; (ii) that such an avowal says nothing against the practical value of the utterance as a message of fact.

[3] Note the caution suggested by this word to our interpretation of *οὐ κατὰ Κύριον.* He certainly does not mean that he is silly, but that he wishes them to listen to him as if he were, if they will listen. Anyhow, *ex pari* (equally), he does not ask them to take the words as inspired; he does not say the Lord has no connexion with them.

[4] See ix. 4.   [5] lit. 'if anyone does', 'whoever does', and so throughout.

[6] oratione utor injuriis et contemptu formatâ (**I am using reference to damaging language and studied insults**).

apostolic footing. But it is not really so. **No** (δὲ); **on whatever ground anyone** in question **dares,** stands up boldly for himself, **(in foolishness I say it)** there **I dare too.**   Let us go over the points.

Ver. 22. **Hebrews are they,** these self-assertors, claiming to come from the inner circles of traditional Jewish life and faith? **So am I. Israelites[1] are they?** Men who claim full place in the theocratic nation? **So am I. Seed of Abraham are they?** claimants by pedigrees of his great inheritance of blessing? **So am I. Messiah's**

Ver. 23. **agents are they?** Do they claim a special connexion with the great Messiah, οἱ Χριστοῦ 'men of Messiah', διάκονοι Χριστοῦ, working servants of Messiah? **(I speak a mad word,** for the facts are too strong for cooler language). **I am** that and **more.[2] In toils more overflowingly, in prisons more overflowingly,[3] in stripes overwhelmingly, in death often;** such have been the surroundings (ἐν) of my

Ver. 24. 'agency of Christ'. To proceed; **from Jews five times[4] I took forty-save-one** (Deut. xxv. 3); **thrice[5] I was beaten with sticks,** bastinadoed; **once I was stoned;[6] thrice[7] I**

Ver. 25. **was wrecked, a night and a day I have spent in the deep,** clinging to a spar; **at travels[8]** often, **at dangers of rivers,** flooded and

Ver. 26. swift, **dangers of brigands, dangers from kin,[9]** from Jew, **dangers from heathens, dangers in town, dangers in wild, dangers at** (ἐν) **sea, dangers in sham brethren's** company;

Ver. 27. **by toil and moil,[10] in sleepless nights often, in hunger and thirst, in lack of food often, in cold and nakedness;** and then, to mention one thing more on the head of all the rest—**apart**

Ver. 28. **from the extra matters,[11]** the things which I might dwell on but do not,[12] there is **the pressure on me** (ἐπίστασίς μοι), **the daily** pressure, **the thought-and-care,** the anxiety, **for[13] all the churches,** all the mission stations planted in my circuits in Asia Minor, Macedonia, and in your own Achaia. All over that vast surface of life

---

[1] See Trench *Synonyms of New Testament*, § xxxix; Lightfoot on Gal. vi. 16; note on Phil. iii. 5 in *Cambridge Greek Testament*. Note Phil. iii is a close parallel.

[2] Of course no man could be 'more' than the Lord's minister, in one sense. But yet he was the 'agent' in a way which made mere 'agency' too small a term to cover his call to act and suffering.

[3] So R.V. as to order.   [4] Unknown occasions.

[5] Unknown.

[6] Acts xiv. 19.

[7] occasionibus non nobis notis **(on occasions not known to us).**

[8] dativus respectus **(retrospective dative).**

[9] The generic article is often omitted as we omit it.

[10] 1 Thess. ii. 9; 2 Thess. iii. 8.

[11] Otherwise with R.V. and A.V. 'the things without', i.e. those hard circumstances of my lot, objective.

[12] Sans parler d'outres choses **(without speaking of other things).**—Segond.

[13] Or perhaps occasioned by, arising from: Matt. xiii. 22. les soucis que me donnent toutes les Eglises **(the anxieties which all the churches give me).** —Segond.

Ver. 29. and work I am in touch not only with communities but individuals; **who,** of all the converts anywhere, **is weak,** is ill, physically or spiritually, **and I am not ill,** too, in sympathy? **Who of** them all **is stumbled,** hindered in his Christian life by vice or error, **and I am not on fire,** with pain for the sufferer, and indignation over the cause, even as now in your case?

But, stay. This is an enumeration of his achievements. He will pause.[1] There is another side, a side of utter humiliation (almost grotesque), but which also makes him out as the genuine emissary of the Lord.

Ver. 30. **If glory I must** any longer, **the** details **of my weakness I will glory of;** the things where I have been made indeed to look a fool for Christ. I say it in awful earnest. **The God and Father** Ver. 31. **of the Lord Jesus knows, the God who is blessed unto the ages, that I am not lying.**[2]

Ver. 32. Take one example. **In Damascus the ethnarch,**[3] an officer **of Aretas the King, was guarding the Damascenes' city,** Ver. 33. **to seize me** (omit θέλων). **And through a window in a basket I was lowered, through the wall, and clean escaped his hands.** Such unheroic incidents have marked my course; I have been treated like a bale of goods in the course of labour for my King.

We make no attempt in this chapter to insert any detailed comment. We may note, however, that the Apostle gives us in conclusion an example, a singular and striking one, of the side of his labours and sufferings which we venture to call the unheroic side, in a certain sense—the incident of Damascus and the rope-basket (σαργάνη). That was an adventure which might have befallen the least creditable of people, and in that respect belonged to the ἀσθένειαι of the apostle, things which viewed from a mere criticizing standpoint might speak either of the coward or the knave. It is only in connexion with his willingness to face and to record such an incident, in relation to his all-absorbing life-work, that it throws—as it clearly does—a light on the profound reality and urgency of his life-call.

---

[1] se colligit (**he gathers himself**).   [2] Gal. i. 20.
[3] ἐθνάρχης was used of the head of the Jews in Egypt and of the Jews in the time of Origen in Palestine. May it not be the same here? There were 10,000 Jews in Damascus. Cf., of course, Acts ix. 22-25.

Chapter xvi

ST. PAUL'S APOLOGIA—HIS INFIRMITIES

2 Corinthians xii. 1-10

A SLIGHT pause of thought seems to mark the opening of Ch. xii. The Apostle is still engaged in his 'glorying', in other words, in the emphatic statement of the credentials of his apostolic mission and authority, as they are presented through his personal experiences. So he proceeds, still in the same line, but now on a loftier level. He will 'glory' still, and still in a deep connexion with 'infirmities'. But the infirmities are of a kind which, while abundantly full of humiliation, are yet dignified by intense suffering; and they are occasioned, as he will explain, by a previous experience of grace and glory which sheds a solemn light over the whole. Still, the key-note is, 'my infirmities' as moral evidence of my apostolate; humiliation as guaranteeing my claims on your attention and obedience. And with this final most remarkable statement in that direction the long καύχησις, begun xi. 22, shall close, before he comes to the final messages of the Epistle.

Ver. 1. **To glory I am bound,**[1] it is not my choice, but my necessity, under the circumstances; **true** (μέν), **not a beneficial thing,**[2] not a direct means, certainly of spiritual benefit either to you or to me, but a duty in order to clear the way to openings for blessing; as it may be necessary to cross a malarious belt to reach a region of health and beauty. Not beneficial, no; **but** (δὲ) it must be, and so, in the course of the process, **I will come to visions and unveilings**[3] **of the Lord,** granted, wrought by the Lord,[4] in the annals of my life, and which adequately guarantee, if you trust my word about them that I am indeed nothing if not His messenger. **I know**[5] **of a man,** you need not ask his

Ver. 2. name, a man **in Christ,** in living union with Him, and now as it were swallowed up in Him, **fourteen years ago and**

---

[1] Following the R.V.
[2] Cela ne convient pas (**that would not do**).—Segond. But is this right?
[3] ὀπτασίαι developed.
[4] Cf. Gal. i. 12 for construction and Rev. i. 1.
[5] Not 'I knew'.

more, (such is the date in that man's story I am about to narrate,[1]) **whether in** the **body I do not know, or out** of the **body**[2] **I do not know—our God knows—raptured,** I say, **such a man,** the person so described, this man in Christ, **as far (up) as the third heaven,**[3] speaking of that unseen world in terms of this, as to place and direction,

Ver. 3. as we must; **and I know of the man in question,** the man thus described, **whether in** the **body or apart from** (χωρὶς) the **body I do not know—our God knows—that he was raptured**

Ver. 4. **into the Paradise,** the very abode of the Blessed and of their Lord with them (Luke xxiii. 43). What he saw there I do not say, but he was there, **and heard unutterable utterances,**[4] (not unintelligible, but) **which it is not lawful for human being to speak;** such was their secrecy, such their connexion with a world of final holiness and bliss, (and perhaps) such was their bearing on the privilege

Ver. 5. and coming glory of the hearer. **Over a man like this will I glory;** glory in the sense of boldly claiming for him a divine mission. (I don't say, over myself; looking at the conditions of that rapture; truly it was 'not I': **no, over myself I will not glory** in connexion with such experiences, **but only** in regards of **my weaknesses;** *there* I may speak personally enough.) But to resume, I will, with that

Ver. 6. reserve, after such an experience, glory, affirm my mission. **For if I shall claim** (θελήσω), now or on coming occasions, **to make a glorying** (aorist), **I shall not be a foolish man** for doing so; it will not be a baseless act; **for I shall** but **speak truth,** the truth of facts. **But,** I do not press this now, **I spare** such words, **for fear anyone in view of me,** apart from my Lord, **should reckon,** should make estimates of what I personally am, **beyond and above what he sees me to be, or what he hears from my lips.** In other words, I *might* dilate much more on that amazing Apocalypse, and its inferences as to my mission. But such a line would tend to lead you to think less of the mission and more of the man; as to the *man,* I want you to take me just as I am in presence and speech, not as the subject of a heavenly rapture, **as** it were out of myself.

Let us pause here to make a few brief remarks on the character and contents of the verses which we are paraphrasing and of which we are making a running exposition in this chapter.

---

[1] Was it at Lystra? Acts xiv. 19.
[2] Cf. v. 8.
[3] Cf. Eph. iv. 10, 'all heavens'. We have seven heavens in *The Testaments of the Twelve Patriarchs,* Levi § 3 and in the Talmud. But here, surely, we have no such enumeration. It may be 'heaven of spirits' as beyond that 'of clouds' and 'of stars'. On Paradise see J. Lightfoot on Luke xxiii. 43.
[4] O homo valdè dilecte! (**O man greatly beloved!**).

As regards contents, we have been led boldly and abruptly into the supernatural as an element in the writer's personal experience. He who had previously told us about broken nights, and short provisions, and swollen rivers, and church-anxieties, and the basket slung from the window, now, in the same tone, has just told us about a rapture into the third heaven, in paradise, and the hearing there of unspeakable words. And he is about to proceed in the same tone to narrate an experience of suffering in which a personal spiritual agent of evil is concerned, and which is followed by explicit colloquies between Paul and the exalted Saviour, which seem to be meant in a sense quite literal and matter of fact.

As regards character, different readers will take the paragraph (vv. 1-10) no doubt in very different ways. To some it will be the utterance of a visionary, or at best of a man liable to fits, so to speak, of nervous illusion. Others, and I hope we shall be among them, will see the life and experience of St. Paul as too much of a piece, too vast and consistent a total, to admit of such a view. It seems to us far more credible that supernatural experiences of the soul of man should after all be possible, and be at times absolute facts, than that the man presented to us at large in the Acts and the Epistles should have been capable of extreme delusion precisely in connexion with ideas and influences which lay plainly at the heart of his life, and that life not only so wonderful but so profoundly practical. Paul's apostolic life is suspended on his conversion, which he repeatedly and in circumstances of the utmost publicity affirmed to have been supernaturally conditioned, I mean as to its outward circumstances. The life is a powerful witness to the genuineness of its alleged first moving power, and its far-sighted practicality is a powerful evidence to the large sanity of the man who narrates the supernatural starting-point of it. Well, but if that starting-point was supernatural fact, then there is absolutely nothing *in kind* in this paragraph which is not perfectly credible. The rapture to paradise, the unspeakable words, the messenger of Satan, the colloquy with Christ, are no more abnormal and no less credible than the light and the voice from heaven outside Damascus. To Paul they were absolute facts;

and they may be abundantly so to us, too, as we look at Paul *in toto*.

Let us take the paragraph, then, as eminently a revealing paragraph of this most human of Epistles. It delivers to us facts of the Unseen, to be received, to be believed, as information through an authentic messenger of God. It delivers to us that the world we see not yet is a real world; that a third heaven is; that paradise is; that the human spirit can be consciously there, can there hear and understand. It delivers to us the existence of personal agents of evil, capable under permission of assailing even the flesh of man. It delivers to us the reality of prayer, and of the attention of Christ to it. In the sphere of purely spiritual experience it delivers to the Church for ever the fact of the sufficiency of the grace of Christ to meet the whole need of the tempted.

Such is the character and such are the contents of the paragraph—which yet springs directly out of the incidental and the personal, and came up because Paul had to substantiate his apostolate, in the way not of formal but of moral evidence at Corinth.

Let us listen to him now as he speaks of his weaknesses. What follows on that supreme and beatific hour to which he has just referred?[1] A tremendous trial, now to be recorded.[2] All, however, be it noted in the way of evidence of his apostolic claim. For He who scourged him thus did it because he was His implement, and He must keep him unspoiled for His work.

Ver. 7. **And in regard** of, **by the vastness of the revelations, (therefore), to preclude my self[3]-exaltation, there was given[4] me, as the allotment of my Lord, a splinter[5] for to pierce the flesh,** a tremendous infliction in my physical feeling;[6] which, as to its incidence and management, was, like Job's awful malady, the action of a spirit of evil, (so I was made to know) and thus it may be called, **Satan's angel,** sent **to buffet me,** to belabour me with blows

---

[1] Cf. the Sequel to the Transfiguration.—(Ed.).
[2] So R.V. divides and renders ἐξ ἐμοῦ, καί.
[3] This practically renders ὑπερ.
[4] Rev. xiii. 5.
[5] σκόλοπες ἐν τοῖς ὀφθαλμοῖς Num. xxxiii. 55.
[6] What exactly we shall never know.

which seemed meant to crush my work and my energy, **to preclude**
my self-exaltation. It was a terrific experience of humiliation,
Ver. 8.   and of strain upon faith. **Over this,** about this, **three times**[1]
to my Lord did I appeal that he, this messenger of evil, **might with-**
draw from me,[2] and let me breathe and work again.[3] **And**
Ver. 9a   **He has said to me,**[4] with an answer which stands good for
me now as then (perf.), **Sufficient for thee is my grace;**[5] **for power**[6]
such as thou needest **in weakness gets completed** (τελεῖται). 'It is
only under the discipline of self-despair that thou wilt fully use me'.

Most sweetly, therefore, for if He thus spoke it is logic enough for
Ver. 9b   me, **will I glory by preference in my weaknesses,** basing
my hopes, and joys, and claims rather on my sense of nothing-
ness and impotence than on my recollections of achievement, **so that**
there may be spread over me, as **tabernacle,** as a Shekinah, **the**
power of our Christ;[7] 'so that it may'; for it will do so more and more,
Ver. 10.   the more I realize and *avow* my absolute need. **Wherefore I**
feel deliberate complacence in weaknesses, in outrages,
in needs, in persecutions, in straits (tight places), **on Christ's behalf,**[8]
in His service, over His work; **for whenever I am weak,** then, just then,
I am strong, I am able; it is when I ask Him to be my all, in the confidence
of self-despair, **then** for all things **I have power**[9] (Phil. iv. 13).

'Sufficient for thee is my grace', or as the familiar Authorized
Version has it—'My grace is sufficient for thee'. This, as we have
seen, is a word spoken by The Lord Jesus, in and from His
glory, to a disciple still wrestling along the path of the pilgrimage.
As such it is one of a precious series preserved to us in the New
Testament. We have words so spoken by that speaker to Saul
at his conversion (Acts ix. 4-6), to Ananias at Damascus (ix. 10-16),
and to Paul again at Corinth (xviii. 9, 10), in the Temple (xxii.
18-21), and in the Roman citadel at Jerusalem (xxiii. 11). But of

---

[1] more Domini **(after the fashion of the Lord).**
[2] A. Monod (*St. Paul* § 5) thinks it is 'that He' in his afflictive pressure
'would stand back', and hold His hand.
[3] Monod has some noble remarks on the wonder it was to St. Paul to pray
thrice without a 'Yes'.
[4] Stat verbum **(His word stands thus).**
[5] 'Enough for thee the grace of Me!'
[6] Omit μου but see below.
[7] Phil. iv. 13.
[8] ita gloriatio illa (cap. xi) justificatur: non se sed Christum extollit **(so that**
glorying (ch. xi) is justified: he does not lift up himself but Christ).
[9] τότε δυνατός εἰμι ἐν ᾿Αυτῷ!

them all surely none is more precious, more pregnant of 'comfort and good hope through grace', more full of the unutterable heart of Jesus, than this.

It comes to us, as we have seen, as part of a narrative of personal spiritual experience. We should know nothing of it had not St. Paul opened us this holy secret of his soul, and told the Corinthians, and told us through them, of that crisis (fourteen years ago when he wrote) of awful need and of wonderful deliverance. Let us not take up this treasure lightly. It is a sacred thing, not only in itself, but because of our getting it through this personal disclosure and confession. It was with a great effort, probably, that the Apostle told the Corinthian converts about 'the thorn in the flesh', 'the angel of Satan', and about his three imploring appeals to the Lord to be set free from the intolerable trial. Deep souls (and St. Paul's indeed, was one) do not lightly open up their secrets. The more let us reverence and prize the gift when, as here, for our sakes and for the Lord's glory, the effort is made, the sacrifice of individual feeling is offered up.

In regard to what was 'the thorn'—a whole literature has been written on it. But for us now it matters not what it was. Enough that it was, to a very strong man, a tremendous trial; a something which for the time darkened his whole spiritual sky; a conflict which brought him face to face with the powers of hell.

He cried out for release. 'I besought the Lord thrice that it might depart'. He records the repeated entreaty without any regret, with no trace of a feeling that he ought to have endured in silence. '*Lerne zu leiden ohne Klagen*' ('Learn to suffer without crying out') is a noble precept—as regards 'cries' to man, which are often better forborne. But the maxim has no bearing upon cries to God, to the Christ of God. Too ready, too outspoken, too confiding, we cannot be in 'telling Jesus all'. Such 'crying out' will not weaken us; it will only strengthen us. For it is the outgoing of our soul not only to infinite kindness, but at the same moment to infinite wisdom and strength. It is taking refuge in the Rock. It is 'coming to the Living Stone'. And that (1 Pet. ii. 4, 5) is the way to become 'living stones' ourselves, by contact, by contagion.

So 'he besought the Lord thrice'. He was answered. There was a divine attention and response. The Lord, once Himself

driven to 'strong crying and tears', Himself once a suppliant in a
yet darker hour, asking, in the profound simplicity of pure human
agony, for the 'passing' of the 'cup' of unknown sorrows, quite
understood His servant. It must have been a help to the servant,
heart-broken with the struggle, to reflect that he appealed to
One who once said Himself (Psa. lxix. 20), 'Reproach hath broken
my heart'. St. Paul could be sure, then, as we may be sure now,
of that Friend's supreme 'acquaintance with grief'. Yet the
answer was not, in form, an affirmative, a consent. The thorn
was not willed away; the 'evil angel' was not driven back into the
deep. As in Gethsemane, so with the Apostle in his dark hour,
there came not a consent to the request in detail, but the meeting
of it with a transcendently higher blessing. 'Thorn', and 'angel of
Satan,' might, or might not, be ultimately withdrawn. But then
and there in all His fullness, in His all-sufficient present Self
(for 'grace' is just the Lord of all love and power Himself, in
action for us), Jesus Christ was given to this saint. In the power
of that gift the saint found on a sudden that the dread adversity
had changed its character and position. It was not upon his head,
overwhelming. It was beneath his feet, overcome. It has been
transformed into 'an occasion', not 'of falling', but of 'mounting
up with wings'. 'I take pleasure in distresses, that the power of
Christ may rest upon me'.

'As then, so now'. That ear is not heavy today, nor that arm
shortened, nor that grace less sufficient. Nor is the assurance of its
sufficiency couched less distinctly now than then *in the present tense*.

The story has often been told (it is authentic; it was the experience of a great servant of GOD recently in our midst) of the
agonized suppliant who, as he cried with tears, 'Let Thy grace
be sufficient for me', lifted his wet eyes and saw upon the wall,
lately hung there, the words, 'My grace is sufficient for thee'.
The '*is*' was painted bright and conspicuous, and it caught his
eye and filled his heart; and he rose up, there and then, to a new
life of peace and power.

Yes, it is true today. It is an everlasting present tense.

'It *is* sufficient', and 'for thee'.

Chapter xvii

SUMMARY AND RE-STATEMENT

2 Corinthians xii. 11-21

St. Paul has concluded his long and wonderful utterance beginning with the recitation of ancestral privilege, and of heroic labour and suffering, passing thence abruptly to the grotesque escape from the Syrian enemy, thence to the heaven of heavens, thence to the splinter and the fiend, and so to the power of the overshadowing Lord in His servant who, at the last gasp, quits self for Him. Here with the apostle we may pause awhile; only to note the profound human interest of the whole passage we have paraphrased, along with its divine authority and message. All is steeped in human feeling and human relations. It is the substantiation by an imperial envoy—by an inspired Apostle—of his commission from the Throne, his *right* to be credited and obeyed at Corinth. How is it done? Not by the cold assertion of certain premises and the formal statement of certain conclusions. Paul pours out his heart to hearts which knew him well enough to know, in their depths, that he is neither a fraud nor a fanatic. And so what he does is just to depict his missionary life and to uncover his profoundest personal experience, and then to ask them—am not I ὁ Χριστοῦ, Christ's own man, and His man for you? Is not your first missionary no mere adventurer but the Lord's ambassador? He had, behind it all, a definite commission from the King; 'He is a chosen vessel to bear my name'; 'I send thee far hence to the nations'. But he is a man, full of soul, and full of affections; and he prefers to accredit himself, taking *that* for granted, by as it were throwing open his robe and showing apostolic wounds.

St. Paul now begins to sum up, and to re-state points, as he draws to a close. In the concluding passages of the Epistle we have the paraphrase with little additional comment, so that we may the better attend to the words of the Apostle himself.

Ver. 11. **Have I proved a foolish person**[1] after all[2] in this long strain of personal assertion? **You**[3] **forced me into it. For I**[4] **had a claim to be authenticated,** attested in my position and rights **by you; for** in **nothing did I fall short of the superlative apostles,**[5] **even though nothing I am;** this I have amply reminded you of. My personal deficiences, of presence, of utterance, may be what you please; I am willing to own myself *nothing* in that sense. But that leaves the

Ver. 12. evidence for my *commission* quite untouched. **The signs,**[6] the tokens, **of the Apostle**[7] **were worked out,**[8] actualized, **among you,** assuredly, when I was with you, whatever your previous ideas[9] of the *personnel* of an apostle might be; yes, they were present **in fullest** (πάσῃ) **persistency,** in a persevering course of ministry; **by**[10] **signs,** and **wonders, and acts of power.**[11, 12] Surely you had your full share of such events in the history of your evangelization; you could not complain that wonders had marked the history of e.g. Galatia or of Asia, or of Macedonia, but that of Achaia was commonplace. **For what**

Ver. 13. **is it in which you were degraded** (ἡττήθητε) put in a lower class in this respect, **beyond the other churches—unless indeed** in the fact **that I personally, did not come down as a burthen on you,** impose myself on you, for pecuniary support? *That I must* plead guilty to; I can only humbly plead, **forgive me this injustice!**[13] But, indeed, I am impenitent here; I shall do it again!

Ver. 14. **Look, I am in the act, now** (τοῦτο) **for the third time, of coming to you;**[14] and now, as before, **I shall not impose myself** (omit ὑμῶν); I shall not ask for a penny; **for I am not in quest of your** money, **but of you;** you, for the Lord, and under Him for us, that is, for His full Gospel. And is not this just what I ought to feel,

---

[1] Interrogative, or Indicative?

[2] Omit καυχώμενος.

[3] Emphatic.

[4] Also emphatic.

[5] xi. 5.

[6] Emphatic. μὲν has no δέ expressed, but it is understood. See below.

[7] As it were, the species of apostle; as when we say, 'He is the missionary all over'.

[8] Rom. xv. 19.

[9] δέ (understood).

[10] Omit ἐν.

[11] 1 Cor. i. 31 (pro constructione) **(for the construction).**

[12] Cp. for δυνάμεις:—1 Cor. xii. 10; Matt. xi. 20. Collocated, as here, 2 Thess. ii. 9. Cp. St. Paul's allusions to his miraculous powers:—Rom. xv. 19 (parallel expression); 1 Cor. xiv. 18 tongues.

[13] ironica amicissima **(irony most friendly).**

[14] The translation leaves unaffected the ambiguity of the Greek. Was it a third readiness, or an actual third arrival? Great are the difficulties attending an actual visit from Asia before the writing of this Epistle. This phrase is *slightly*, in its context, *for* it. See Appendix D.1.

claiming as I do to be your spiritual father. **For there is no claim**
Ver. 15. **on the children to hoard for the parents; no, it is on the
parents for the children.**[1] But I will not measure my
obligations to you even so; it is not only to spend on you that I am ready;
I shall be delighted to spend, aye, but more, I shall be delighted **too**
myself to **be spent to the** (ἐκ-) last of me, **over your souls, if,** as it appears, **loving**[2] **you more overflowingly I am loved less**; in other
words, if my devotion to you hitherto is so ill requited, it only the more
determines me to the more entire devotion, till you *must* be overcome.

Ver. 16. But I know there are cruel insinuations even in the face of these
avowals of disinterested affection; insinuations that I have
done by others what I would not do direct. **But granted,**[3] (it may be
put thus), **I**[4] **did not** personally **impose myself on you;** no, **but being
essentially** (ὑπάρχων) **an unscrupulous person,**[5] 'a born rogue', **by
craft I took you;** using others as agents and blinds to make a profit out
Ver. 17. of you. Who were they? **Did I** (μὴ) use thus **any of the men I
have sent to you**[6]—**by him,** I say, **did I fleece you?**
Ver. 18. **I appealed to Titus** to visit you on my behalf, when I wrote
my first apostolic letter; the visit to which I have referred so
often; **and I gave joint commission** with him to **the brother** whom
you know;[7] how, **did Titus fleece you at all? Was it not by the
same Spirit,** under the leading of the same Holy Ghost, **that we
walked,** behaved and acted? Was **it not in the same footsteps?**

Ver. 19. But here I pause; a truce now to the explanations. **You have**
(πάλαι) **long been thinking,** I feel sure, **that we are vindi-
cating ourselves to you,** as suspected criminals before a court of
enquiry, anxious to make the best of an uncomfortable case. Believe
me, it is otherwise. Our consciences are clear before God. And our
painful thought is that it may soon be *our* part to act as a court of enquiry
among *you*. **In God's direct presence** (κατέναντι Θεοῦ), **in Christ, are
we speaking;** not in the fear of man, but in the fear of Him, which
gives truth, candour, and courage. **But all** these (τὰ) **things** which we
do speak, **dear friends, are for the sake of your building up**[8] in
Christian life and love; these supposed 'excuses', these careful vindi-
cations, are said not in nervousness about our claims but in order, by
retaining your confidence in our assured mission, to keep you strong,
Ver. 20. and help you to grow spiritually. Here we *are* anxious; we
feel you need it sorely. **For I am in fear, lest somehow on**

---

[1] pulchrum (**beautiful**).   [2] Omit καὶ, retain ἀγαπῶν.
[3] ἔστω δέ.   [4] I emphatic.
[5] ita loquitur! (**so it is being said!**).
[6] q.d. μὴ οὕτως ἀπέστειλά τινα ὧν κ.τ.λ.
[7] An allusion not to be confused with the ἀδελφός of ch. viii.
[8] Cf. x. 8.

arrival I should find you not such as I wish you to be, **and I should be found as to you not such as you wish**[1] me to be **lest somehow** it should be all **strife** (sing.) **animus** (sing.)—jealousy—**heated feelings, partisanships, defamations** (not necessarily backbitings), **whisperings, swellings, disturbances; lest on my coming** Ver. 21. **back**[2] **my God should humble me in view of you, and I should have to weep for many of those who have sinned ere now,**[3] **and** yet who **never repented over the impurity, and fornication, and lasciviousness which they committed.**[4]

A pause, a sad and solemn one, marks the end of Ch. xii. The Apostle's thought has revolved again, and with deepest feeling, towards the darker side of the Corinthian position; his ἀπολογία has taken a turn which forces on him the thought that most painful elements of difficulty and of sin await him in the mission-church. For the time, the happy thoughts generated by the response made to his appeal for the Jerusalem Fund retire into the distance; and he can think of nothing but the deplorable work of the new propaganda of οἱ Χριστοῦ, and of the willing ear evidently lent to them by many of his old converts.

Nor only this. The last paragraph of Ch. xii is occupied not so much with *that* feature of the position as with what we may call the *libertine* element in the mission, to which he had referred above, e.g. vi. 14-vii. 1. He anticipates, when he shall be with them again, the sorrow of finding not only divisions, party spirit, recriminations, and the like, which, of course, the influence of οἱ Χριστοῦ could account for, but 'many' a converted who was impenitent still in such matters as impurity, fornication, and wanton living. This was not the direction which, with all their errors, the influence of οἱ Χριστοῦ would take; a somewhat strict religious discipline of life would, at least on the surface, mark the programme.

Here, then, is the Apostle's heart still obliged to ache over mischief, not subdued, however reduced, at the opposite pole. With that deep sigh, that groan of loving pain, he pauses at xii. 21.

---

[1] q.d. οἷόν με θέλετε εἶναι.
[2] See Appendix D.1.
[3] 'The perfect indicates the abiding stain of the fact if not annulled by repentance.
[4] Ver. 21: cor eloquitur (**his heart speaks out**).

Chapter xviii

CONCLUSION

2 Corinthians xiii. 1-14

THE closing chapter of the Epistle forms a fairly distinct division as regards its contents. At xiii. 1 St. Paul resumes his utterance with a somewhat altered tone, yet in deep inner continuity. The sad prospect is still before him. But he faces it with the thought not of the anguish he will suffer when he comes but of the firm and stern measures which he must inevitably take, if things then prove to be as he fears. There must be investigation, and action. Oh, that they would yet forestall it by a vigorous *self*-scrutiny and *self*-reform! All he has written, all he now threatens, is only for their good; he will rejoice if they leave him nothing to do as examiner and reprover. And so, he bids them in the Lord farewell.

We return to the rendering and concluding paraphrase, leaving the chapter to speak for itself.

Ver. 1. **For the third time now I am coming to you.**[1] And when I come it will be my painful duty to hold a regular and rigorous enquiry. '**At the mouth**[2] **of two witnesses and of three,**' now one, now the other, in legal form and with legal fullness, '**shall be settled every case,**' every utterance, as it is brought up for cognizance; charges of wrong by word or by deed will all be strictly dealt with.[3]

Ver. 2. **I have given due notice, and I am giving it** now again, **—as when present with you the second time, so while yet absent now**—notice, I say, **to those who have previously sinned,** to all and sundry who will then stand accused of committed transgressions,

---

[1] xii. 14. Does this mean a third visit or a third resolve and preparation? But see the next verse. Also Appendix D.1.
[2] ἐπί with genitive, as if 'depending on the mouth'. Matt. xviii. 16 perhaps quoted here. But both go back to Deut. xix. 15.
[3] Judicis partes sustinebit et testes arcesset (**he will assume the part of judge and will summon witnesses**).

123

and to the rest of you without exception, for all need warning, **that if
I do come on a return visit**—a re-visit—'to the back again'—**I shall**

Ver. 3.   **not spare;** I shall not act with false leniency towards proved
offenders. I say this to meet the disloyal demand that I should
give practical proof of my inspired mission, as if it were doubted; yes,
practical proof shall be given if needful, in this sad way; **since you are
seeking a test of** the reality of **the Christ who in me**[1] **is speaking,**
as against that phantom-Christ to whom the other side appeal as their
watchword; the Christ who in me speaks the message of salvation and
of holiness, and **who towards you is not weak, but is powerful
among you.** Yes; if you will but think, He has proved Himself no
mere theory at Corinth. As preached by me He has been, and in measure
still is, no uncertain influence on your souls, yea, a mighty power in your

Ver. 4.   community; a Saviour and a Lord shown to be *alive* indeed
by His blessings. **For He was crucified as a result of
weakness;** yes, it is true; like us His servants He gave Himself up
helpless, to His persecutors, though it was a weakness sublimely voluntary and for a purpose; **but He lives, as a result of God's power;**
lives with a life which is the result of that uttermost feebleness, as it led
Him to the moment when the Father, accepting His sacrifice, called Him
triumphant from the tomb. And the Master is now, in a sense, repeated
in His servants. **For we are weak,**[2] we like Him bear the appearance
of personal feebleness, and yield ourselves to adverse circumstance,
in Him,[3] in the life of union with Him; so that even our 'weakness'
has a sacred side; **but we shall live,**[4] we shall prove to be alive indeed,
with victorious energy, **with Him,** as side by side with our risen
Lord in our action for Him, **as a result of God's power,** working in us
to will and to do, **in regard of you,** in whatever we may need to do, in
apostolic authority, for Corinth.

The reference, it will be observed, is not to the life spiritual,
eternal, or of the resurrection; but to life in its aspect of energy;[5]
'mine enemies live, and are mighty' (Psa. xxxviii. 19). This by
way of interjection.

---

[1] Emphatic.
[2] Secundum nos ipsos (**as far as we ourselves are concerned**).
[3] Some read σύν. The meaning is closely akin.
[4] Sc. vivida ac strenua actione (**Sc. with activity full of life and vigour**).
[5] Cf. i. 6, 10. The theme in the opening verses of the Epistle re-appears
as it draws to a close. There as here the Apostle is 'restored to life and power
and thought' for his ministry.—(Ed.). See further Appendix D.3, third
paragraph, p. 158.

We return to the paraphrase, leaving our final rendering to make its own impress, sweet and solemn, on the reader, as it did on its own first Christian audience in Corinth.

Ver. 5. Well, but cannot this be forestalled? Oh, that it might be, by your own action. **Put yourselves**[1] **to the proof,** not waiting for our inquest, **whether you are in the faith,**[2] whether you are indeed believing truly on the true Saviour, and living the life of faith in Him; **test yourselves**[3] so that we may have no need to do it. **Or do you not recognize yourselves,** have you no spiritual insight into your own state, **that Christ Jesus is among you,**[4] that you need no other Gospel, no other Saviour, than Him whom Paul first taught you, for by His blessings in your life He proves His nature and His presence? Can you not see this? Oh, surely you can—**unless indeed,** awful alternative, **you are** somehow **reprobate,**[5] rejected after test, proved base metal, no Christians at all in the true sense. **But I hope that you will know,** will see, when we come, **that we are not reprobate,**[6] that *our* Christianity is not a counterfeit, void of purity, and power; no, you will find us living and real, for joy or sorrow. But oh, dear friends, our hope and prayer is that, at any cost to our reputation it *may* be to your joy.

Ver. 6.

Ver. 7. **But we are praying** (εὐχόμεθα) **to our God that you may do no ill (at all);** that both in general and in this particular case of readiness for the enquiry you may act so as to be perfectly clear; not for the sake of *our* reputation, that *we* may come triumphantly out against our opponents, as you submit, and obey, and give up inconsistencies at our appeal; **not that we may appear the genuine article,** may have the κῦδος of full recognition as Christ's ministers, **but that you may do the honourable,** right **thing, while we shall be in a sense** (ὡς) **rejected;** in other words, our prayer is that you may so reform every defect ere we come that your Christian position may be unassailable, for the pure sake of God's holy will, even though this will *ipso facto* reduces us to the inaction and apparent stultification of opening a commission when there are no delinquents to appear before us.

Ver. 8. For in a sense we should then have no power to exercise. **For**

---

[1] Emphatic.
[2] It is doubtful whether ἡ πίστις here is the equivalent of the Creed.
[3] Emphatic.
[4] Ergo vivite Christiane (**therefore ye live as Christians**).
[5] Counterfeits.
[6] Sc. quod revera apostolica potestate praediti simus (**Sc. for we are endowed with real apostolic power**).

we have no power, no judicial authority, **against the truth, but only on the side of the truth**; the faithful believer and liver is out of our range; our only commission is *for* the Gospel and its practice *against*

Ver. 9.   error and evil-living. Such an 'impotence', such a reduction *ad nihilum* as to formidable authority, is only our delight. **For we are only happy whenever,** in *this* sense, **we are weak, while you are powerful;** when we have not a word to say, not a bolt to hurl, because you are strong on the vantage ground of unassailable truth and holiness. **This**[1] **is what we are actually praying for—your perfection,**[2] your faultless adjustment and equipment for the fullest Christian

Ver. 10   life, which we could only admire and love. **It is on this account,** and for no lower motive, of person or of party, **that I am writing from a distance,** on purpose that when I am **on the spot I may not have to deal severely, using the authority which the Lord gave me**—for He gave it me for ends of blessing, not of mischief, **for building up,**[3] **and not for demolition.** Its ἔργον is the former; its 'strange work' only is the latter.

Ver. 11.   **To conclude, brethren, farewell (and hail).** Get yourselves perfected. **Perfect yourselves,** in individual and social fullness of holy obedience and love; **be encouraged** in a new departure of Christian life; **be one in heart,**[4] in sentiment, purpose, aim; **live a life of peace; and the God of true** (τῆς) **love and peace will be with you,** your eternal Companion and Friend. **Greet each**

Ver. 12.   **other with holy kiss,** the salute of endeared friendship in

Ver. 13.   the Lord. **You are greeted**[5] **by all the saints** who are around me here.

Ver. 14.   **The grace of our** (τοῦ) **Lord, Jesus, Messiah,** of Him whom *we* have preached to you, **and the love of** our **God,** His sublime affection for you His children in His Son, made real to your hearts, **and the participation of the Holy Spirit,** a full share to each of you, and a common and mutual enjoyment by all of you, of His indwelling and His power, **be with all of you.**[6]

---

[1] Omit δέ.
[2] Cp. Luke vi. 40; Heb. xiii. 21.
[3] xii. 19.
[4] φρονεῖν e.g. Col. iii. 2; different from φροντίζειν.
[5] Construction inverted.
[6] Subscription: noteworthy only as naming Luke with Titus.

APPENDICES

WISE MEN AND SCRIBES

There is one word of our divine Lord's which has often, in the life and labour of a religious teacher, been a help and cheer to my thoughts. It is found in a dark context, in the twenty-third chapter of St. Matthew; but it has a pure ray of light to shed upon vocation in a University, 'Behold, I send unto you scribes.'

He speaks in the same sacred breath of sending prophets, and of sending wise men to act, and also if need be to suffer. But the word I fasten upon is, 'I send unto you scribes'; the men of the library, the book, the pen, the teacher's chair. Their function lacks from many aspects the possible grandeur of the life which is called into the field of open action for the Lord; the life for example of the pastor or of the missionary. As one has said, it is the life whose business is rather to sharpen the sickles of others than to go out armed into the standing corn, and reap, and reap, till the evening comes, and with it the call home to the reward.

Nevertheless, the life of the scribe is a life that is capable of mission; 'I send unto you'. And that is enough to furnish matter for devotion and hope.

—The Inaugural Lecture.

See also *Christ's Witness to the Life to Come*, Sermon VIII.

APPENDICES

APPENDIX A

Biographical

To obtain a full impression the official biography needs to be read—*Bishop Handley Moule*, by J. B. Harford and F. C. Macdonald (Hodder and Stoughton, 1922). The notice in the Dictionary of National Biography which is given here is probably new to many readers. What Dr. Lock has left us is a remarkable miniature, showing how Bishop Moule appears in the portrait gallery of his contemporaries. We have added some fresh biographical observations with special reference to Dr. Handley Moule's work on 2 Corinthians. It may also be stated here that in the home circle his life was better than a sermon, and his chief characteristics were humility and humour. As Bishop he was much appreciated as a witty and humorous after-dinner speaker, and on a variety of occasions. His name is a memorial.

HANDLEY CARR GLYN MOULE (1841-1920), Bishop of Durham, was born at Fordington, Dorset, 23rd December, 1841, the eighth son of the Rev. Henry Moule (q.v.), by his wife, Mary Mullett Evans. From home, where his father educated his sons and other pupils, a home full of scholarly and literary as well as of religious and missionary keenness, Handley Moule passed to a brilliant career at Trinity College, Cambridge (1860), being bracketed second classic (1864) and elected fellow of his college (1865). He also read for the voluntary theological examination, but 'the distressing pains involved in the mere growth of thinking' had raised doubts in his mind, and he hesitated to be ordained. From 1865 to 1867 he was an assistant master at Marlborough College. Then, mainly through his mother's influence, all hesitation vanished: he was ordained at Ely. He first acted as his father's curate at Fordington, keeping in touch with Cambridge, where he gained for several years the (Seatonian) prize for a sacred poem. Recalled in 1873 to Trinity, he acted as dean, being also curate at St. Sepulchre's Church, until 1877, when his mother died, and he returned home until his father's death (1880).

At that moment the Evangelical party in the Church of England was planning the erection of Ridley Hall at Cambridge as a theological college for ordinands: Moule accepted the Principalship, and held it for nineteen years. He married in 1881 Harriot Mary, daughter of the Revd. C. Boileau Elliott, F.R.S., rector of Tattingstone, Suffolk, by whom he had two daughters. This was a period of great happiness and influence: his wife was in whole-hearted sympathy with his aims; he won the devoted allegiance of colleagues and pupils; he preached regularly at Trinity Church, and often before the university; inspired and guided many religious movements in the university; spoke often at Keswick Conventions and Church Congresses, and published numerous books. In 1899 he was elected Norrisian Professor of Divinity, and, while professor, was brought into close touch with the leaders of other sections of the Church by taking part in a round table conference on the doctrine of the Holy Communion, impressing them much by his spirituality, and being impressed by them.

In 1901 Moule was appointed to the See of Durham. As a bishop his strength lay in his personal and spiritual appeal; he was in touch with clergy and laity alike, with quick sympathy for all suffering, with charity to those who differed from him, an enthusiastic leader in all missionary effort and in preventive and rescue work. Rather un-English in temperament—of French ancestry on his father's side, of Welsh on his mother's—he was naturally timid and highly-strung, but his whole life was one of persistent development in power. He became fearless in asserting the truth, unruffled in the face of difficulty and sorrow, deepened and even brightened by the sorrows of later life, when he lost a daughter and his wife. But, while growing in power and in toleration, he remained unchangingly within the limits of the faith as he had learnt it in his father's house. He wrote much—treatises theological, devotional, exegetical, biographies, poems, hymns —notably, *Outlines of Christian Doctrine* (1889); *Thoughts on Christian Sanctity* (1885); *Veni Creator* (1890); *Charles Simeon* (1892); *Christus Consolator* (1915); *Philippian, Colossian, and Ephesian Studies* (1897-1900). His writings form the most spiritual and scholarly expression in his generation of the Christian faith as held by Evangelical churchmen, proud of the Reformers, and holding that their teaching is 'the most loyal in proportion and emphasis to the New Testament standard'. He died at Cambridge, 8th May, 1920.

(Bishop Handley Moule's *Memories of a Vicarage*, 1913; J. B. Harford, *Letters and Poems of Bishop Moule*, 1921; J. B. Harford and F. C. Macdonald, *Handley C. G. Moule, Bishop of Durham. A biography: with bibliography*, 1922.)

W.L.

A scholarly and sympathetic biographical sketch has also been written recently:—*H. C. G. Moule*, by Bishop Marcus L. Loane, M.A., formerly Principal of Moore Theological College, Sydney (Great Churchmen Series No. 1: Church Book Room Press). The episcopal period still awaits adequate treatment and authoritative assessment. In the official bibliography there are 175 works detailed, and the catalogue at the Bodleian Library contains some 200 entries.

The Warden of Keble, Dr. Walter Lock (1846-1933) was himself a native of Dorchester. He was also a pupil at Marlborough when Horace, Charles (Senior Classic) and Handley Moule (Second Classic) were assistant masters. He may, therefore, be regarded as a product of the teaching of these remarkable brothers, of whom Horace was generally regarded as the most brilliant.

It will be seen that Dr. Lock's record takes much account of the family life and background, and very rightly so. Dr. Trevelyan has stated that 'an examination of the facts will show that the great men of letters . . . who made the fame and fortune of the early and middle Victorian age had been brought up with more variety and freedom, either at home or at day schools or small academies . . . where the wheat and tares were for better and worse allowed to grow up, each in their own way, until the harvest'.[1] In this regard Handley Moule may be thought of as

---

[1] *British History in the Nineteenth Century* (1922). G. M. Trevelyan, p. 172.

one of the last of the great Victorians—good grain gathered in in the last hours of harvest home. It is instructive to note that Handley Moule in his farewell sermon at Fordington in 1880 referred to that occasion as 'the deepest change and greatest crisis which, as regards outward things, ever has come, or is ever likely to come, into my life'. This sermon only exists in the original MS., but a portion of it will be found at the end of Ch. III in the present volume.[1] That course of the life of Handley Moule which was seen and best known, therefore sprang from the hidden spiritual spring of the family home life at Fordington.

In point of chronology it will be seen that his life falls into two periods each of nearly 40 years duration. The first was chiefly associated with Fordington, and the second with Cambridge and Durham. It is in the middle of this latter period we must take note of his work on 2 Corinthians as Norrisian Professor (1899-1901). These few but significant years, falling almost exactly in the middle of the second part of his life, were at once an epilogue after nineteen years at Cambridge and a prologue to the last nineteen years at Durham. His work on Second Corinthians was therefore the completion of his detailed work on the text of St. Paul's Epistles while he was at Cambridge. But it was also a providential preparation against personal afflictions and the heavy incidence of episcopal responsibilities at Durham.

Dr. Lock emphasizes the fact that out of weakness he was made strong, and there is no doubt that he himself connected this with a particular occasion, when, in an act of definition, he laid personal claim through faith to the all-sufficiency of God's grace in all things. From the point of view of spiritual development the rest of his life may be regarded as a resolute retention and progressive occupation of that vantage ground of personal faith. The occasion is described in the official biography, p. 128, and he duly noted the date in his diary every succeeding year of his life. There is a

---

[1] See pp. 17, 18. The passage is from the conclusion of the sermon, and the verses may be found in The *Life*, p. 63.

[2] (I believed, Sept. 18, 1884; Parkhall. Thanks be to God!).

Readers may refer to the present volume, p. 93. The homiletic comment after ix. 8, is found in the MS. of The Lecture Notes. His 'Morning Act of Faith', which follows, is an extension of the sentiments recorded in the margin of his Greek Testament.

reference to this in his *Greek Testament* where, against 2 Corinthians ix. 8, he has written *Credidi*, Sept. 18, 1884: *Parkhall. Deo Gratias!*[2]

During the episcopal period, when there was a clearing of correspondence, it was a joy to him to turn to literary composition. It was his intention to retire in August of the year in which he died. In this case we may picture him taking up his old notes, as he sometimes did, for re-writing and working in new directions —old notes on this wonderful epistle, which had been the subject of his lectures twenty years earlier as Norrisian Professor. What a treasury he might have left us of rich, ripe spirituality and pastoral leadership! Yet in such cases of foreshortening we may humbly hope that, in the inscrutable purposes of Providence, God has 'provided some better thing for us, that they without us should not be made perfect.'

APPENDIX B

The Inaugural Lecture

THE Inaugural Lecture was entitled 'An Inaugural Lecture'. Delivered in the Divinity School, October 13, 1899. By H. C. G. MOULE, D.D., *Norrisian Professor*. The occasion is given in the *Life of Bishop Handley Moule*, by Harford and Macdonald, Ch. XIII, and there is the following entry in the diary:— '*Oct.* 13, *Friday. Morning*: last preparations for Inaugural Lecture. To the schools at 11.10. Large and kind gathering. Delivered Lecture with merciful help'.

The passages in the lecture relevant to the Epistle are these:—

'The choice of this particular Book of the Holy Scriptures, the Second Epistle to the Corinthians, was determined in my mind by several considerations, On the whole, that Epistle has been comparatively speaking, somewhat neglected, as a field of study in itself. Yet few great portions of the New Testament have a more distinctive character—I might almost say, so living are its pages, a more powerful individuality. No doubt it cannot be studied without frequent reference to its great predecessor, the First Epistle, written so short a time before, and attached to it by so many links. Yet in important respects the Second Epistle stands apart, a thing of its own kind, full of phenomena peculiar to itself.

'In two directions in particular this wonderful document may give us, in this its individuality of character, a specially useful field for study. If I do not mistake, a difficulty often felt by younger students in the theological school, applying themselves to the New Testament, is the difficulty of so reading the Epistles, particularly of St. Paul, as adequately to grasp the often subtle and complex sequences of thought, and to present to themselves in a satisfactory way the complete drift and argument of extended passages. Careful and excellent work is often spent upon what is commonly called "Introduction", with its problems of genuineness, authenticity and integrity. Minute attention is given to main variations of reading. Vocabulary and grammar are often studied with true scholarly care and skill. Nevertheless, sometimes, with all these preparations, a certain disappointment is felt as to the hold which the student has got upon the whole document, or on its parts, as living utterances, written before all things to be understood, in their bearings and connexions. It is my hope that the Second Epistle to the Corinthians may be found an exceptionally useful exercise for that sort of attention which is resolved not to be content without a satisfactory hold upon the writing in its genuine drift and purport. For in few of the Epistles, if any, are the connexion and argument, often and again, so fine and subtle in their texture, or again so veiled and clothed, as it were, with personal emotion; and nowhere meanwhile is it more important to seek for them, to divine them amidst the concealments, and to set them out before the mind. My readings will be aimed very much in that direction.

'The necessary topics of "Introduction" will not be neglected. Happily in this case what is really necessary for our purpose in that direction need not long detain us. Something must, of course, be said about date, and main occasion; and there will be need to take notice of the rather complex question of "lost Epistles" and unrecorded apostolic visits; and questions have been raised, not indeed (in the least degree of importance), about the Pauline authorship of any part, but about the integrity of the Epistle as it stands, about the possibility of a part or parts of it having been originally a distinct document. But all this may be noticed so as to assist private study, and yet all be kept subsidiary to the main purpose, the subject-matter and its mental and spiritual texture. Introduction may, and I hope, will, be kept altogether subordinate to Interview.

'Such, then, is one aspect in which I hope to find this wonderful writing a fruitful field for students of the New Testament—its aspect as a writing in which attention to drift and sequence is constantly demanded.

'Then in another respect it will, I think, prove itself a subject-matter of special significance. It presents, as it seems to me, in singularly powerful form and vivid colour, an example of the distinction and the harmony of the human and the divine in Holy Scripture. It is on the one hand a letter, written by a man; the free and versatile expression, eager, wistful, even burning with complex emotion, of a profound and sensitive human heart. It is on the other hand an oracle, charged with inestimable truths of Revelation, for sure and authoritative conveyance to our faith. Under the first character it offers itself as matter not indeed for merely intellectual study; for nothing which is fully human can be fully studied by the intellect alone. But it invites a study the same in kind as that which we should bring to epistolary literature in general, to the letters, for example, of Pliny, or Julian, or Bernard, or Luther, or Scott; the study which will seek to apprehend the links of thought, the play of feeling, the irony, the pathos, the contrast, all the methods of impression. From this point of view we shall need to banish to the best of our power all merely conventional associations of the word "Epistle", and regard our document as simply as a *Letter* as if it had been received through the post today. Most surely we shall then see exemplified the fact that the literary messengers of the Eternal Spirit were given not only *some* liberty for the movements of their own being, but a liberty full and magnificent; they were not merely still *themselves*; they were lifted to be themselves in the highest measure. Under the second character we shall approach the Epistle with a religious and reverent attention, in which spiritual insight must do its proper part, and in view of which the student is sure to go wrong if he ever forgets the need of an illumination not his own, and the need of prayer that it may be given. For this Letter, written with the amplest human freedom as a Letter, is so managed, by One to whom our freedom is all the while His implement, that it is an Oracle, too. It is written by a man who was all the while "a chosen vessel to bear the Name" of our salvation. He is in the hands of God for that purpose; to convey to our faith and hope the message of supernatural truth, the express revelation of the heavenly Master. He affirms himself to be such, and to act so, again and again, notably in the Galatian Epistle; and he does so there in terms which leave us the alternative of thinking him to be either the victim of an immense and mastering illusion, or the prophet of Almighty God, sent to us with an articulate Gospel by the Christ Himself.

'As we study the Letter, we shall pursue from one vivid paragraph to another the mind of St. Paul; so he thought, so he reasoned, so he wrote. As we study the Oracle we shall reverently ask to know what his Lord has to speak through him. Over the utterance so listened to we shall say,

"Thus stands it written".

'Most certainly we shall not always be able to analyse and explain clearly to ourselves the distinction, in every great passage, of the aspect of the Letter and the aspect of the Oracle, and their relation to each other. But we may hope, so the study is with the whole heart, and done as in the divine presence, to apprehend enough of both to give us a growing sense alike of the historical and human reality of the document, and of its inestimable and divine trustworthiness for our life and for our death.

'I have ventured thus far to indicate, in somewhat general terms, the aim and aspiration with which I would approach the Biblical subject of my intended readings. There is little need to say that the task is in itself one to contemplate with more than misgiving, when the lecturer considers himself. But if there is any work upon which a man, believing himself lawfully called to it, may dare in his need hopefully to beseech divine light and aid, while he brings to it all he really can of his care and labour, it is surely the work of academic exposition of the Holy Scriptures. That work must always present its marked and important differences from the expository treatment intended primarily for spiritual edification. It is imperative of course that it should give an attention to the literary and historical sides of the subject-matter which may lawfully be left out of the other work, at least to a large degree. But then the academic exposition, from a Christian chair, is nothing if not aimed ultimately at the right use of Holy Scripture for not its secondary but its supreme purposes. So far as it deals with "Introduction", historical, grammatical, or whatever it may be, it must remember that Introduction (may I repeat the remark?) is altogether for the sake of Interview, and of the sort of Interview which can only be rightly entered upon in reverential faith'.

The Lecturer then concluded with a characteristic reference to Matt. xxiii. 34: 'Behold I send unto you—not only "prophets and wise men", but—"scribes". The men of the library, the book, the pen, the teacher's chair: and the life of the scribe is a life that is capable of mission; "I send unto you"' (see p. 129).

The Lecture was well received. Professor Gwatkin wrote: Thanks for the Inaugural. It is the right note, and I am further glad of it, because I think our Cambridge School is getting too much absorbed in prolegomena and literary details and needs a call to higher and wider things, which it is in some danger of leaving undone'.

Bishop Moule stands as a significant figure in the middle of the stream of the classic Evangelical succession. His teaching on the Atonement can be seen in this volume in Chapter VIII, which deals with a passage from the Epistle which he himself describes as a cardinal passage for the determination of this doctrine (v. 11-21). His teaching on the Inspiration of Holy Scripture is implicit in the words above from the Inaugural Lecture, and his views may be taken as authoritatively representative of his own school of thought.

In connexion with the Evangelical doctrine of Inspiration we may well refer to Bishop Westcott's summary of the *Primitive Doctrine of Inspiration*. Bishop Westcott, writing of the early fathers, says:

'They teach us that Inspiration is an operation of the Holy Spirit acting *through men*, according to the laws of their constitution, which is not neutralized by His influence, but adopted as a vehicle for the full expression of the divine Message. . . . They teach us that Christ—the Word of God—speaks from first to last; that all Scripture is permanently fitted for our instruction; that a true spiritual meaning, eternal and absolute, lies beneath historical and ceremonial and moral details. . . . It is possible that objections, more or less serious, may be urged against various parts of the doctrine, but it cannot, I think, be denied that as a whole it lays open a view of the Bible which vindicates with the greatest clearness and consistency the claims which it makes to be considered as one harmonious message of God, spoken in many parts and many manners by men to men— the distinct lessons of individual ages reaching from one time to all time'.[1]

It will be seen that Bishop Westcott's summary of the Primitive Doctrine approximates very closely to the Evangelical Doctrine as expressed by Bishop Moule in his Inaugural Lecture. Though growing always in appreciation of the view points of others these convictions remained with Handley Moule to the end. 'Heaven and earth shall pass away: but my words shall not pass away' (St. Mark xiii. 31). AMEN *non intelligo sed credo* (AMEN I do not understand, but I do believe), he writes against the text in the margin of his Testament. The Word of God was for him at once wholly human and fully divine—Holy Scriptures because written word for word and full of human sentiments, but also absolutely Holy because altogether God-breathed, the inspiration in his own phrase, '*descending to the phraseology*'.[2]

What this signifies verbally, so that variations are seen to be moving parts of a living organism, can perhaps only be fully appreciated by application to the actual details of autograph MSS. We are unable to do this in the case of Holy Scripture; for the original autographs no longer exist. Yet we may learn much through thoughtful study and work on other sacred writings. The Inaugural lecture only exists in print, but we still have the autograph of the Lecture Notes, and some of the impressions borne in upon the mind of the Editor after his work may be seen at the end of the Appendices which follow. (See below pp. 145, 149, 152. Also the Extended Note at the end p. 160).

---

[1] Westcott, *Introduction to the Study of the Gospels.* Appendix B. On the Primitive Doctrine of Inspiration .

[2] This authentic fragment of Bishop Moule's teaching I received more than 30 years ago from my immediate uncle, the Ven. W. S. Moule, who was a student at Ridley Hall, 1885-1887. He also attended Bishop Westcott's lectures, learning much from his immense reverence for the text. On the inspiration of the phraseology see further *Extended Note—Coalescent Inspiration*, p. 160.—(Ed.).

APPENDIX C

Manuscripts and Authorities

THREE chief sources are used in the editorial composition of the present volume—*The Lecturer's MS.*; *The Bishop's Greek Testament*; and *The Other Writings*. It will be convenient to deal with these in order, in each case also describing briefly, not only the authority, but also the historical circumstances of its composition, and the way in which it is used in the present work.

1. THE LECTURER'S MS.

This is the main source of the book, and is of considerable literary and historical interest. The official *Life*, Ch. XIII may again be consulted for details. The MS. was kept in a large envelope and written in ink, except for occasional pencil corrections later, and consists in all of 175 pages of exercise paper, pinned together into sections. These may be grouped as follows:

(*a*) PREPARATORY. Being admitted Professor on 29th April, 1899, the author remained at Ridley Hall till near the end of August, making preparations for the future. The subject of 2 Corinthians had evidently been chosen early. But exactly how early it is not possible to say, as the diaries are missing. The first available entry is *July* 25: 'Reading in 2 Cor.', and from this time the entries show that the work of preparation was done periodically from morning to morning. The result of this work of preparation is seen in the first 24 pages of the MS. The first page is headed, '*Materials for the Corinthian Problem from* 1 *and* 2 *Cor.*'. The Epistles are worked through verse by verse, quotations and observations are written out, and at the end the '*Results of the Collectanea*' are summarized. None of this preparatory material has been used.

(*b*) THE LECTURES ON INTRODUCTION. No further work was

done in September, when the author was on holiday, and engaged in settling into his new home at 5 Salisbury Villas and into his rooms at St. Catharine's, at the end of Sept. and early in Oct. The Inaugural Lecture was finished on Oct. 7, full term started Oct. 10, and the Inaugural Lecture delivered on Oct. 13 in the forenoon. The same evening the first lecture was given on 2 Corinthians. *Oct.* 13: 'To Catharine for evening lecture—many—adjourned to Hall'. The Introduction seems to have been completed in three or four lectures and the MS. covers 11 pages. These lectures are written out in note form only. The Introduction in the present volume is therefore reconstructed from lecture notes and contains editorial matter. (see also p. 151).

Together with the Introduction we must place detailed notes on the problem of the unrecorded visit, which are represented in Appendix D.1., p. 154.

(*c*) THE FIRST TERM LECTURES. The lectures were delivered on Wednesday and Friday mornings at 11.10, in the Divinity Schools through the term. *Oct.* 18, *Wed.*: 'Lectured at 11.10. Perhaps 50 there'. *Nov.* 24, *Frid.*: 'Lecture (last), 2 Cor'. The first page of this part of the MS. is headed, *A Paraphrastic Summary of 2 Cor. with primary reference to connexions of thought*, and there are 43 pages. The summary is at first very brief. For instance, page 1 includes 2 Cor. i. 1-11. With ver. 12, however, a system of brackets is introduced, which helps to distinguish the actual translation, which is a careful rendering of the Greek, from the paraphrastic additions which are largely designed to show the connexions of thought. The translation has been rendered in this volume in heavy type and the paraphrastic additions in ordinary type.

From Ch. i. ver. 1 to Ch. iv. ver. 15 it has been necessary, partially, to reconstruct the translation and paraphrase, but rapidly less and less as the lectures proceed. As the author had more time for preparation his treatment became more detailed, and from Ch. iv. ver. 16 he gives us a fully completed translation and paraphrase. There are also a certain number of notes included in the MS. which have been put as footnotes, except as in

Ch. VIII where they are put at the end. The first term lectures are represented in Chs. I-IX of the present volume. It should, however, be noted that there are no prose sections in these earlier lectures. The prose and homiletic sections in Chs. I-IX are supplied from the author's other writings, as can be seen later (Section 3, p. 150: *Table of Editorial Material*, p. 153).

(*d*) THE SECOND TERM LECTURES. During the Christmas vacation there is no record of any work on the Epistle. The author was engaged on his *Ephesian Studies*. *Jan.* 8: 'Work at Ephesians—fair progress'. *Jan.* 17: 'I wrote much at Ephesns., and find in evg.'. As term approached he was at work on 2 Corinthians again. The following entries are of interest: *Jan.* 23, *Tues.*: 'Prepd. for lecture—Lectd. (1st for Term) at 11.10. Abt. 20 there.' *Jan.* 25, *Thurs.*: 'St. Paul. Lecture, 11.10. Increased no., good time'. *Feb.* 14, *Wed.*: 'Mg. worked at 2 Cor.'. *Feb.* 15, *Thurs.*: 'Lecture at 11.10'. *Feb.* 16, *Frid.*: 'Spent morning over proofs of Ephesians'. *Feb.* 27, *Tues.*: 'To lecture at 11.10; finished 2 Cor.'. *Mar.* 1, *Thurs.*: 'Lecture at 11.10 (last)'.

The MS. of the Second Term Lectures clearly reveals how much more time and thought the author was now able to devote to the subject. The first page is entitled, 2 *Corinthians, Lent Term*, 1900. *Ch. vii. 2 and onward*, and now there are 97 pages. The MS. begins with a lengthy prose section which is found entire in Ch. X. The reader may see that the titles of Chs. I-IX are all taken from Ch. X, the opening passage (q.v.: page 63). The list of subjects there given has been used retrospectively for the divisions and chapter headings of the Epistle i. 1-vii. 1.

The quotation in the middle of Ch. X from Bernard corresponds with the quotation in the Introductory remarks in *Ephesian Studies*. The whole of the treatment of this second part of the Epistle contains periodic explanatory prose sections, all of which have been included. The translation and paraphrase are dealt with more fully than in the first half. The brackets are now discarded and the free translation is henceforth underlined to distinguish it from the paraphrase, as for instance in the case of the author's *Expositor's Romans*, the MS. of which is still extant. There are also more frequent notes, all of which have been incorporated. From this point onwards use is made of the French translation of Louis Segond.[1]

The Second Term's lectures are represented in Chs. X-XVIII. Editorial use has been made again of passages from other writings, but in view of the prose sections available this has not been done so extensively as in the first part. Ch. XV contains no additional material and represents the MS. very much as it stands in the second half of the Epistle.

The Editorial work has, of course, included a great deal of disentangling, rearranging, and deciding which cannot be described at length here. Obvious words may have been supplied; a choice sometimes must be made between two parallel words in the MS., one in ink another in pencil; indecipherable comments are omitted; references may have been re-arranged, or completed; and so forth.

One interesting and exceptional example may be quoted. Ch. iv vs. 2 the MS. has the two bare words—So λίβανον. The rest of the footnote is therefore an editorial deduction (see p. 27, iv. 2 footnote[1]).

In dealing with these manifold details the conviction grows that some at least of our difficulties in understanding the nature of verbal inspiration might be resolved if only we could realize more fully that we are dealing with holy writings—not Holy 'Printure', or Holy 'Typeture' but Holy *Scripture*, all written originally by hand and then repeatedly transcribed, before ever they were put in print.[2] It is all too easy to forget this elementary, primary and basic fact, and work on an autograph is perhaps the only way in which we can fully realize what inspiration means. The fixity of print and the typewriter inevitably conveys a sense of impersonal and stereotyped finality, which is altogether foreign to the flexible and written word. But to engage in handwork on an autograph is to work hand in glove with the author.

---

[1] *La Sainte Bible, qui comprend l'Ancien et le Nouveau Testament, traduits sur les textes originaux hebreu et grec,* par Louis Segond. Imprimerie de l'Université: Oxford, 1880. This translation may be obtained from The British and Foreign Bible Society.

[2] See title-page for the *quill.*

2. THE BISHOP'S GREEK TESTAMENT

Bishop Handley Moule was Norrisian Professor for just over two years (1899-1901). In the summer of 1901 he was on holiday at Beatenberg in Switzerland, and on Aug. 11 received from Lord Salisbury a letter with the offer of the See of Durham. His letter of acceptance was dated Aug. 17, and a full account of this transitional period may be found in *The Life of Bishop Handley Moule*, Pt. II, Ch. 1. 'Called to the Episcopate.' The enthronement took place on All Saints' Day, Nov. 1, 1901, and he preached on 2 Cor. iv. 5. This sermon is printed in *My Brethren and Companions*, Ch. XIII, 'The Pastorate of Service.' Against the text in his Greek Testament he has marked: '*My text*. Nov. 1, 1901. Amen'.

At the end of 1901 the Bishop's nephew, Dr. H. F. Moule, who was then at work on Darlow and Moule's catalogue of printed Bibles for the British and Foreign Bible Society, presented the Bishop with a copy of Nestlé's Greek Testament. The title is: *Novum Testamentum Graece cum apparatu critico*, curavit Eberhard Nestlé. Editio tertio recognita. Stuttgart: 1901. (*Greek New Testament with critical apparatus under the care of Eberhard Nestle. Third revised edition. Stuttgart*, 1901). The fly-leaf has Dec. 1901 inscribed as the date of the gift.

This Greek Testament was the Bishop's constant companion for eleven years—at Bishop Auckland, about the diocese, in the train, and on holidays—and it was his habit to record with a neat pencil note the date when he began and when he finished each book. The first entry in the Testament is: *Adsis Domine mi* (Be Thou present, O my Lord). *Begun July 29, 1902, at Auckland Lodge*. The first entry against the Second Epistle to the Corinthians is Nov. 6, 1903, and the Epistle on this occasion was finished Dec. 13, 1903. On the last occasion he read the Epistle in the Testament the opening entry is Jan. 30, 1913, *Westbourne Terrace*, and the closing entry Jan. 31, 1913—a pause being made overnight, presumably in the middle at vii. 1. The concluding entry at the end of the Testament is Mar. 16, 1913, *Palm Sunday*.

At the top of each page of his Testament the Bishop has put, in Latin, his own succinct summary of the passage. None of these headings has been used in this volume, so that it may prove of value for the sake of completeness to set them out in order here. They give a good idea of the general style of the Latin notes and provide devotional scholarly summaries of various important passages, and of the whole Epistle. They may even suggest subjects for Exposition. The references indicate the portions of the Epistle allocated to each page in Nestlé's Greek Testament:

i. 1-4: Ep. altera—Exordium. i. 5-12: Pastor pro grege et patitur et consolationem habet—Simplicitas. i. 13-ii. 1: Se vindicat contra crimina mutabilitatis—Dominus Amen est. ii. 2-16: De peccatore iam paenitenti restaurando. ii. 17-iii. 10: Epistola commendatoria—Littera et Spiritus. iii. 11-iv. 4: Evangelium nullo velo eget, utpote mansurum. iv. 5-17: Norma et vires operis apostolici—Spes victrix. iv. 18-v. 12: Domus non manufacta—Spes et ambitio Christiana—Timor Dni. v. 13-vi. 4: Evangelii cor: Christus pro nobis peccatoribus mortuus et vivus. vi. 5-17: Litterae Ordinationis! Separatio Christiana. vi. 18-vii. 9. Potentia promissionum—Titi adventus sedat Apostoli anxietatem. vii. 10-viii. 3: Titi relatio de animo Corinthiorum—Collectio pro sanctis pauperibus. viii. 4-17: Exemplum Macedoniae. viii. 18-ix. 4: Titum aliosque fratres laudat—Excitat Corinthios ad largiendum. ix. 5-14: Dnus ditare potest Corinthios ut alios ditent et ita gloriam Dno augeant. ix. 15-x. 12: Hortatur Corinthios ad se recipiendum, ut qui in bonum eorum a Dno missus sit. x. 13-xi. 7: Corinthus legitime Pauli κλῆρος est—Pauli anxietas de errorum progressu. xi. 8-22: Pauli abstinentia ab omni stipendio ap. Cor—'Gloriari' vult. xi. 23-xii. 3: Gloriatio apostoli de doloribus et laboribus, de humiliationibus et visionibus. xii. 4-14: Agonia apostoli post visiones—'Sufficit tibi!'—Iterum compellat Cor. de animo suo erga eos. xii. 15-xiii. 3: Se vindicat de simplicitate animi —Metuit ne Cor. inveniat minime Christianos. xiii. 4-13: Admonitio, spes, amor, salutatio, benedictio.

(i. 1-4: The Second Epistle—The beginning. i. 5-12: The shepherd both suffers and has encouragement for the benefit of the flock.—Candid sincerity. i. 13-ii. 1: He clears himself of charges of fickle vacillation—The Lord is the Amen. ii. 2-16: Concerning the restoration of the sinner now a penitent. ii. 17-iii. 10: Letters of commendation.—Letter and Spirit. iii. 11-iv. 4: The Gospel needs no covering, in that it will last. iv. 5-17: The standard and strength of apostolic labour—Hope the conqueror. iv. 18-v. 12: A house not made with hands—Christian hope and ambition—The fear of The Lord. v 13-vi. 4: The heart of the gospel: Christ for us sinners, dead and alive. vi.·5-17: Letters of Ordination! Christian separation. vi. 18-vii. 9: The power of the promises—Titus' arrival allays the Apostle's concern. vii. 10-viii. 3: Titus' report of the attitude of the Corinthians—The collection for the poor saints. viii. 4-17: Macedonia's example. viii. 18-ix. 4: He praises Titus and the brethren in general—He rouses the Corinthians to give freely. ix. 5-14: The Lord is able to enrich the Corinthians, so that they may enrich others, and thus increase the glory which is the Lord's. ix. 15-x. 12: He urges the Corinthians to accept himself as one who has been commissioned by the Lord to see to their good. x. 13-xi. 7: Corinth is lawfully Paul's portion—Paul's concern at the advance of departures from the truth. xi. 8-22: Paul's restraint from all pay from the Corinthians—He is disposed to 'Boast'. xi. 23-xii. 3: The apostle's boast of his sorrows and labours, his humiliations and visions. xii. 4-14: The apostle's agony after his visions—'Enough for thee!'—Again he makes the Corinthians understand his feelings towards them. xii. 15-xiii. 3: He champions his own singleness of mind—He is apprehensive lest he find the Corinthians by no means Christians. xiii. 4-13: Admonition, hope, love, greeting, blessing.)

In addition to these cogent Latin headings, rendered into English as best we can, the Greek text is underscored in pencil, certain brackets and signs are used, personal marginal notes are inserted, mostly in Latin, occasionally in French or English, and references added or the printed marginal references underlined. The underscoring of the text is of devotional value. Here, one feels, are pathways worn by the feet of a saint.[1]

This, however, can only be appreciated in MS. and has not greatly influenced the editorial work. The brackets and signs, on the other hand, have proved of considerable value in paragraphing the Epistle, and in other ways. To a large extent they correspond with the Lecturer's MS. The Marginal Notes and references have nearly all been incorporated in the present volume, or used for the development of the author's thoughts. Notes and references will be found in the footnotes. Great care

---

[1] 'I once felt something of this in seeing the Bible of David Sandeman all marked through, and then part of one marked by a lad here, and Mr. McCheyne's Bible I well remember. It was as if you could have read his soul's experience at the time'.—Andrew A. Bonar, *Diary and Letters*, (1893) p. 175.

has been taken to make these refer to the correct point in the text. This, indeed, is one example of the way in which the written word and the printed word can never be exactly identical. But the Editor has done his best to convey to the reader the spiritual signification of the original markings in the Testament.

It will be seen from what has been said that the Bishop's Greek Testament is really the complement of the Lecturer's MS. In dealing previously with the Lecturer's MS. we indicated that light may be thrown on the subject of verbal inspiration by the study of an autograph. In the case of dovetailing the Lectures and the Testament together, with the addition of supplementary material, one is impressed by the possibility of the most intricate editorial treatment of the sacred Text. This, be it noted, without any damage to the most exacting views of plenary inspiration—historical and doctrinal factors excluded. In the case of the present volume passages have sometimes been taken from the Lecturer's MS., sometimes adapted by use of the Greek Testament, and occasionally short Editorial passages composed expanding the thought in one of the marginal notes, or some point in the Lecturer's MS.

Anyone who attempts editorial work of this kind realizes that the work of even a series of redactors is quite possible; and indeed that many parts of Holy Scripture must have had considerable editorial treatment. But when an Editor finds that sometimes he is unable to disentangle his own work, word for word, from the original author, he must be allowed to remain doubtful whether a like feat can be performed with reliable accuracy for the Sacred Text, over a range of thousands of years! In the present case, some readers may like to try to distinguish the first Handley Moule from the second: or is it the third, seeing that the Editor's father (W. A. Handley Moule, 1870-1946) was also the Bishop's namesake?

To live with an autograph is to live with the author, and to live with anyone is to be influenced by their style.

3. THE OTHER WRITINGS

The Lecturer's MS. and the Greek Testament have reference to the free translation and paraphrase, to the footnotes, and to certain prose sections in the second half of the Epistle. The Other Writings have reference to the chief homiletic and explanatory passages.

As we have stated the author lectured on 2 *Corinthians* from Oct., 1899 to March, 1900, during the first academic year of his appointment. In the second year, Oct., 1900 to March, 1901, he lectured instead on *Selected Articles*. The Epistle, however, was not far from his thoughts. In 1900 he was composing devotional studies, several of which were taken from this Epistle. These studies with others were gathered together in the volume, *Thoughts for the Sundays of the Year*. The Preface is dated July 9, 1901, St. Beatenberg, Switzerland—just a month before his appointment as Bishop. The volume contains a variety of subjects but there are found in it studies on the following texts from the Second Epistle to the Corinthians:—iv. 16; v. 8; v. 10; vi. 16.

These passages from *Thoughts for the Sundays of the Year* are, however, not the only passages in the Bishop's writings which have direct reference to the Epistle. He preached at Fordington on i. 20. Before his appointment as Bishop he was preaching at an Ordination Service in Liverpool Cathedral on iii. 6. On the occasion of his enthronement in Durham Cathedral he preached on iv. 5. So that very nearly every chapter in the first half of the Epistle is dealt with in one or other of his sermons. Moreover, all these writings are expository in character, which means that they deal not only with the text but also the context, and often with the general drift of the argument in each particular part of the Epistle.

We see, then, that by a careful study and adaptation of the author's sermons material can be found for the homiletic portions required in the first half of the Epistle. To these have been added other writings of the author, some of earlier and some of later date, but all bearing on the same subject, For instance, there are one or two kindred passages in *Expositor's Romans*. Again there are passages in *Christus Consolator*, from the episcopal period, which deal with themes found in this Epistle. In two cases excerpts have been made from other contemporary authors, in one case where there is a notable coincidence of thought.[1]

The same process of editorial adaptation has been followed in the second half of the Epistle. Here, however, as has been shown, the MS. already supplies a considerable amount of the material required. The *Table of Editorial Material* on p. 153 may be found helpful. The authorities are arranged there according to the order in which they are used and references given to the chapter or page of the book from which they are taken. For further notification of the books used the reader may be referred to the admirable *Bibliography* at the end of the *Life*. Extracts from other authors are placed in square brackets.

A more detailed note may be added on the construction of the *Introduction with a view to Interview*. This has been re-written from the author's lecture notes. The main headings and the general treatment of the material follow the presentation of the subject as set out in outline in the notes. Where there may be consecutive sentences or complete paragraphs these have been reproduced verbatim. Where there are rough notes they have been suitably arranged, and then worked up. A passage from the opening of *Expositor's Romans* has been imported. Occasional editorial use has been made of other contemporary commentators, e.g. Plumptre in *Ellicott's Commentary* (1897), *Rackham on Acts* (1901). A number of Editorial paragraphs based on Scripture have also been composed to fill in the general outline to a considerable extent.

---

[1] Ch. IX. (p. 57-8). The passage is from F. W. Robertson, *Lectures on Corinthians*, and exactly corresponds with the Bishop's sentiments as expressed in the Latin note in his Greek Testament. See also Ch. XI. for a quotation from Denny (p. 71, second paragraph).

In these and other ways the Editor has endeavoured to reconstruct a harmonious whole from the lost chords of the original introductory lectures. The work has illuminated his mind in regard to some of the literary problems of the New Testament itself. Perhaps through his experience others may be enlightened.

Take for instance one problem out of many, that of the pastoral epistles. Are they the work of St. Paul or of a later disciple? Is it not possible that in a very real sense they are the work of *both*? May they not have been written up at a later date from material which the Apostle left behind him, like his cloak and parchments at Troas?[1] In this case the pastoral epistles would have been pieced together perhaps a generation later, but by someone on whom the apostolic mantle had in some way fallen. Yet such was his fidelity, under the inspiration of The Spirit, to the literary remains, and to the ethos of St. Paul and his teaching, that what we have is in effect a series of Pauline epistles which complete the Pauline corpus, a full generation after the Apostle himself had departed to be with Christ.

Is it not a possibility that the 'Problem of the Pastoral Epistles' may be solved in some such way as is here suggested? The reverent study of contemporary autographs may, in the Divine Providence, be used to enlighten our minds concerning the nature and composition of the ancient and Holy Scriptures.

---

[1] I am indebted to Professor F. F. Bruce of Manchester University for the suggestion in this passage.

TABLE OF EDITORIAL MATERIAL

APPENDIX D

Historical Problems

1. THE UNRECORDED VISIT

(from the MS.)

THE case for and against an unrecorded visit of St. Paul to Corinth may be briefly set out as follows.

(A) The Evidence *for* such a visit is to be found in the following passages:—2 Cor. ii. 1: 'I determined this for myself, that I would not come again to you with sorrow' (πάλιν ἐν λύπῃ ἐλθεῖν): 2 Cor. xii. 21: 'lest, when I come again, my God will humble me' (μὴ πάλιν ἐλθόντος μου ταπεινώσῃ με ὁ Θεός μου); 2 Cor. xiii. 1, 2: 'This is the third time I am coming to you' (τρίτον τοῦτο ἔρχομαι) . . . 'if I come again' (ἐὰν ἔλθω εἰς τὸ πάλιν). . . . There is an obvious inherent possibility in such a visit, and when we think of a figure like John Wesley we can the better understand the mobility of such a missionary figure as the great Apostle. But we must remember that there is no absolute certainty in any of the passages cited, and further ask the question as to exactly when such a visit took place.

(i) It may have been before 1 Corinthians was written, i.e. in the long space of three years spent at Ephesus. But, apart from a very doubtful reference in 1 Cor. iv. 18, there is no clear allusion to such a visit in the earlier epistle. 1 Corinthians, moreover, was occasioned by news which apparently came as a painful surprise to St. Paul.

(ii) The visit may have taken place between the writing of 1 and 2 Corinthians, i.e. sometime within at most eight months from leaving Ephesus. If he went from Ephesus itself this seems hardly possible as to time. Apparently he left there soon after 1 Corinthians was written, formulating a plan to go through Macedonia, sending Timothy ahead and then himself making his departure, directly after the uproar in connexion with

Demetrius (Acts xix. 21, 22; xx. i). Perhaps the apostle paid an unrecorded visit from Macedonia. This is quite possible, though also beset with difficulties. For we may ask again, When? Could it have been before Titus' arrival, which we gather was shortly after his entry into Macedonia? (cf. 2 Cor. vii. 5, 6).

(B) The Evidence *against* an unrecorded visit has been given incidentally above. Perhaps 2 Cor. ii. 1 and allied passages are to be rendered of St. Paul's intentions rather than of his actions, and this is the view which we have tried to represent in the paraphrase. The whole of the passage ii. 1f. implies that he was trying to avoid going himself, in order that they should deal with the matter before he arrived. If he had already gone a second time between the writing of the two Epistles he would surely have gone as he indicates in Ch. x. 11, 'what we are in words when absent, such also are we in deed when we are present', and in xiii. 2, 'if I come again, I will not spare'. In this case presumably there would already have been a painful scene, whereas here he is still trying to avoid it. We incline, therefore, somewhat to the view that in three letters he explicitly stated his intention to make a return visit, viz.: (*a*) The original letter (1 Cor. v. 9) in which he stated his intention of coming direct (cf. 1 Cor. xvi. 5, and 2 Cor. i. 15); (*b*) 1 Corinthians (1 Cor. xvi. 5f.); and (*c*) 2 Corinthians itself. 'The third time' in 2 Cor. xii. 14 and xiii. 1 would then refer to his intentions more particularly as expressed in these letters. 2 Cor. xiii. 2 should then be rendered as in the marginal reading of the R.V., 'as if I were present the second time, even though I am now absent'.

We may note that this is the view decidedly held by Robertson (*Hastings Dictionary of the Bible*) who considers the theory of a visit before or after 1 Cor. as beset by hopeless difficulties. We commend the view, therefore, of four Epistles (two no longer extant) but probably one visit.

Together with the uncertainty of an unrecorded visit we must place the uncertainty surrounding the change of plan referred to in 2 Cor. i. 15, cf. 1 Cor. xvi. 5.

2. THE CHANGE OF PLAN

(Editorial)

We are unable to re-construct the precise circumstances of St. Paul's change of plan. But the general situation is fairly clear, and it is a help to remember what he seems to have had in mind in regard to his missionary and pastoral objectives.

As the Apostle said in his first epistle he was a wise master-builder (1 Cor. iii. 10). Therefore we may take it that he sought in his missionary enterprise to work according to a fairly clearly defined plan. It was not sufficient to lay the foundation stone. He must return to see how it had settled into its place and if possible return yet again to make certain that it was still secure. Each visit would be the opportunity of added grace for his converts (2 Cor. i. 15). This method he had already put into operation in regard to the churches founded on the first missionary journey. Each of the churches then established had by now received at least three apostolic visits. But it was otherwise with those more recently founded on the second missionary journey on the mainland of Europe. Living and working at Ephesus (Acts xix) it was still part of his design 'in the Lord' to revisit these churches before he turned back once again to Jerusalem.

As St. Paul, therefore, directed his thoughts westward across the Aegean there were evidently two practical alternatives. Either he could go direct across the sea by ship to Corinth and then work North into Macedonia. Or he could go overland to Macedonia and work down South to Corinth. The former and perhaps easier plan was evidently in his mind to begin with, viz., to make Corinth his base of operations, first working northwards and then retracing his steps. The latter plan—perhaps the more circuitous and awkward from his own point of view—was that which he actually carried out, viz., to go up into Macedonia, work south to Corinth and then retrace his steps from there, as he and Barnabas had previously done from Derbe (Acts xiv. 20f., cf. xx.if.).

What precisely was the cause of this alteration of plans we cannot be quite sure. We may note, however, that having dealt with his great affliction in the first paragraph of his epistle (i. 3-11), he is concerned immediately to pass on to deal in the following paragraphs with motives and movements connected with his change of plan (i. 12f. 15f.). We may therefore conclude that St. Paul's change of plan was in all probability connected in some way with the great affliction which he describes in the opening passage of the epistle.

3. THE GREAT AFFLICTION

(Editorial)

Various theories have been advanced as to the nature of the great affliction which St. Paul describes in 2 Cor. i. 3-11. It may have been the tumult at Ephesus (Acts xix. 23 f.); or Fighting with beasts at Ephesus (1 Cor. xv. 32); or Shipwreck (cf. 2 Cor. xi. 25); or a repetition of infirmities (cf. 2 Cor. xii. 7). The context and phraseology at the beginning of our epistle lead us to think of bodily illness as well as of perils and anxieties, and it may have been accompanied with what we would call today a complete physical and nervous breakdown, following all he had recently been through, including his anxieties over the church at Corinth. His change of plan would be in accord with an experience of acute mental tension, coupled with physical prostration. Incidentally, we may note that when he left Asia, where he had undergone this terrible ordeal, he came straight to Philippi where he would probably find St. Luke the beloved physician (cf. Acts xx. 6).

The influence of St. Paul's affliction on the composition of the epistle may be noted in the following passages. In i. 4-11 he describes the significance of his experience and approaches an account in detail of the actual circumstances. In iv. 1 he returns to a kindred theme, and thoughts of suffering and relief for the

body are never far away in the whole of this extended section
iv. 1-v. 8. It is true that the references are many of them to general
experiences of trial and suffering in the work of Christ. For instance, 'We are troubled on every side yet not distressed; we are
perplexed but not in despair; persecuted but not forsaken; cast
down, but not destroyed' (iv. 8, 9). Here he is evidently speaking
in general of his sufferings for Christ's sake. Yet in the very
next verse he speaks in a way which must have reminded both
him and his hearers of his recent experience. 'Always bearing
about in the body the dying of The Lord Jesus, that the life also
of Jesus might be manifest in our body' (iv. 10, cf. i. 9). The
same theme is carried further in iv. 11 (cf. i. 5, 6). And when we
remember that what St. Paul experienced was something like
a foretaste of the Resurrection of the body (cf. i. 8, 9) then it
helps us to understand how it is that he is led on to speak in
detail of themes concerning the relevance of the body in the light
of the eternal world (iv. 16-18: v. 1f.).

A close and careful reading of the first half of the epistle we
believe will show that his recent experience was never far away
from St. Paul's mind as he composed his letter. In the second
half of the epistle this is not noticeable in the same way. Partly
because, we believe, it was written slightly later, and therefore
what he had experienced had somewhat receded from his conscious
thoughts. Partly, also, of course, because he is dealing with the
practical subjects of the collection and his own defence. We
have, however, in vii. 3, when he resumes, what is, perhaps, an
echo of iv. 12, and towards the end of his apologia the passage
xi. 23-29 may be compared with the earlier passage vi. 4-10.
'Deaths oft' (xi. 23, cf. i. 9, 10) would include his recent experience, so also would 'the things which concern his infirmities'
(xi. 30 and xii. 9). When his apologia is complete, and he gathers
up what he has to say in Ch. xiii, we find a final faint echo of the
earlier theme. Ch. xiii. 4 is a reference to restoration of life in
the sense of energy, just such a miraculous renewal of energy
for spiritual enterprise as he had recently experienced.[1]

---

[1] Vide in loc, p. 124, footnote 5.

We note also that the experience through which St. Paul passed lies only a little in the background of the Epistle to the Romans. We may well believe that his spirit found comfort in expression, and in the long and ordered composition in which he engaged at Corinth.

In conclusion we may note the sequel. St. Paul's great affliction took place, perhaps, on the way to Troas (ii. 12), certainly somewhere in Asia, and it was an experience akin to resurrection (i. 9). On his return journey from Corinth, St. Paul tarried seven days at Troas (Acts xx. 6f.) where he was himself the means of the restoration of the life of Eutychus (Acts xx. 9-12, cf. 2 Cor. i. 3). This great event was the crown of the Apostle's missionary labours in the Eastern Mediterranean.

EXTENDED NOTE—COALESCENT INSPIRATION

'*As thou knowest not what is the way of the spirit, nor how the bones do grow in the womb of her that is with child: even so thou knowest not the works of God who maketh all*' (Ecclesiastes xi. 5).

In its concepts and in its construction every book which has ever been written is the product of growth—growth of thought, growth of words, growth of form and shape. There is nothing new under the sun, and there is certainly nothing new in this.

In the case of the construction of the present volume, however, owing to the nature of the material and the intermittent way in which the work has been carried out, the process and stages of growth have become very clearly marked in the mind of the Editor. In this concluding note a brief attempt is made to apply some of these thoughts of growth to the sacred volume of Holy Scripture; in particular to the question of Inspiration. More particularly, still, to the Evangelical doctrine of Inspiration, which, as we have already seen (p. 141) is in effect the Primitive doctrine of the Church.

According to the Evangelical Doctrine, Inspiration of Holy Scripture is spoken of as verbal or plenary. The word 'verbal' indicates that Holy Scripture is inspired word for word. According to Handley Moule's dictum 'verbal inspiration means that the inspiration descends to the phraseology'. The word 'plenary' (from the Latin *plenus* or full) indicates that the Bible is fully inspired throughout, and that this fullness is also seen even in its details of word and phrase.

In the present note we wish to make the suggestion that a further word should also be considered. Inspiration of Holy Scripture is also 'coalescent', and this word can be added to the other two by way of extension and interpretation. In this case Inspiration is at once 'verbal', 'plenary', and 'coalescent'. 'Verbal' because essentially in words, chosen of God. 'Plenary' because full of inspiration, in detail, and throughout. 'Coalescent' because phenomena of growth are observable everywhere—in words and in books. The three words, being inter-related, are to be held together.

Conservative Evangelical thought may well consider that, theologically speaking, the bane of liberal scholarship has been the obsession of specialists with embryology. Yet every general practitioner must agree that in his text-book embryology has its right and honourable place.

The word 'coalescence' is in originating choice and application our own. But it is also to be found in Canon T. D. BERNARD's book *The Progress of Doctrine in the New Testament*. Quotation has already been made in this volume (p. 65f). We may now add further quotations from the end of Bernard's book.

'Only the written Word of God, confidingly followed in the progressive steps of its advance, can lead the weakest or the wisest into the blessedness of the life that is in Christ. . . . When it is felt that these narratives, letters and visions do in fact fulfil the several functions, and sustain the mutual relations which would belong to the parts of one design *coalescing* into a doctrinal scheme which is orderly, progressive and complete, then is the mind of the reader in conscious contact with the mind of God; then the superficial diversity of the parts is lost in the essential unity of the whole, the many writings have become one Book, the many authors have become one Author' (italics our own).

The characteristic of coalescence is noted by Bernard not only in regard to ideas but also in connexion with the grouping of the books. Again we quote. 'In speaking of the custom of the Church it must first be remembered that the New Testament was not given and received as one volume, but that it grew together by recognition and use. As the books gradually *coalesced* into unity it might be expected that there would be many varieties of arrangement, but that they would on the whole tend to assume their relative places according to the law of internal fitness, rather than on any other principle which might exercise a transient influence. . . . In fact, this tendency shows itself at once in the earliest period to which our enquiries are carried back by extant manuscripts, by catalogues of the sacred books given by ancient writers, and by the habitual arrangement of the oldest versions' (italics our own).

Bernard's words were written a century ago. Broadly speaking, they are in general agreement with the findings of modern scholarship, and remain substantially true today. In Holy Scripture we have indeed an amazing and supernatural power of *coalescence*. This is seen generating from the spiritual power of the events and the ideas which lie behind the writings. It also appears in the gradual growing together and orderly grouping of the various books, each with its own individual unity and internal arrangement.

But, further still. In Handley Moule's dictum, *the inspiration descends to the phraseology* (see p. 141, and footnote 2). Such indeed is the permeation of the potent Inspiration that it can be traced descending through the books and paragraphs right down to the very point where words begin to coalesce into phrases, in expression of the ever varying aspects of the life which lies behind them. As in Nature, so in Scripture, where there is life there is coalescence for the formation of living organism. Where there is life there is coalescence. Where there is no coalescence there is no life.

We cannot explain inspiration any more than we can explain life. But, if we have a right conception, we can the better understand. The view of inspiration here set out helps us to understand several remarkable phenomena in connexion with the Scriptures. If the inspiration does not depend on individual words but rather on their grouping then we can better understand some at least of the variant readings. As we have already seen (p. 145), even original autographs may be far more flexible than we are inclined to imagine. The author's own copy may have contained his own periodic alterations or improvements. We are not compelled to regard it as axiomatic that there is one original autograph of the author, and one only, behind every book. Neither can the distinction between composition and publication have been so clear-cut as it is to-day.

Again, when Holy Scripture is translated it still retains its spiritual power, even when it may not be completely accurate. Why? Not because of the words only, but because of the potent ideas which, through phrases, produce parallel expressions of those ideas in every language.

Yet again, like attracts like. So Scripture has grown. But also, conversely, anything which is *unlike* is incapable of becoming a part of the same organism. The Inspiration of Holy Scripture is perhaps nowhere so strikingly illustrated as in the simple fact that no other writings have been able to find a place in this sacred corpus. Parts have sometimes been severed, as Luther severed the Epistle of St. James, and the body still functions. But no other writings, no matter how sanctified, have ever been able to find a permanent place in the body of those Holy Scriptures which the Church has received to hold.

There is much that could be added by way of expansion and illustration. But our immediate object is to assist in the definition of terms, as distinct from interpretation –physical, moral, or historical.

A right view of inspiration is a basic, vital and, we may add, urgent need in the Church today. The whole superstructure of doctrine is affected by it. The more we can think of Holy Scripture as a corpus, a body, a living organism, surely the greater will be the benefit to the Body of Christ, which is His Church. As Handley Moule has written in another connexion, '*Corporeity after all is a great mystery*'. It is true we cannot comprehend. But we can believe, and on holy ground we are best on our knees.

Almighty and Everliving God,

Who by Thy Holy Apostle has taught us

to make Prayers, and Supplications, and to give Thanks, for all men;

grant, we beseech Thee,

that all they that do confess Thy Holy Name

may agree in the truth of Thy Holy Word,

and live in unity, and Godly love;

grant this, O Father, for Jesus Christ's sake

our only Mediator and Advocate.

AMEN.

ALLELUIA!

I HEARD

A VOICE FROM HEAVEN

SAYING UNTO ME

WRITE

BLESSED ARE THE DEAD

WHICH DIE IN THE LORD
YEA

SAITH THE SPIRIT

FOR THEY REST FROM THEIR LABOURS

AND THEIR WORKS DO FOLLOW THEM

AMEN